YOU CAN'T SHOOT YOUR MOTHER-IN-LAW

The Entirely True Tales
of a Daughter-in-Law

YOU CAN'T SHOOT YOUR MOTHER-IN-LAW

The Entirely True Tales of a Daughter-in-Law

TONYA REID

SYNERGY
PUBLISHING GROUP

BELMONT, NORTH CAROLINA

You Can't Shoot Your Mother-in-Law:
The Entirely True Tales of a Daughter-in-Law
Tonya Reid

Published by Synergy Publishing Group, Belmont, NC
Cover concept by Porter Metzler
Layout and design by Melisa Graham

Softcover, September 2025, ISBN 978-1-960892-53-9
E-book, September 2025, ISBN 978-1-960892-54-6

Dedicated to Billy Reid

You are the best that ever was! It's amazing the way
you love me unconditionally. Especially since you
had absolutely no frame of reference to do so.

Contents

Excuse Me?

"Why, Tonya, you are fatter than I thought you were!" *This* was how my brand-new mother-in-law greeted me as I walked into the kitchen, at her beach house, in my bathing suit.

Out loud. Not just to herself, inside her head. Not even under her breath, to be denied later as a misunderstanding or a gaslighting technique. Not even in an inside voice. She just blurted it out, as if someone had startled her, and the filter between her brain and her mouth had flown off!

"Ma'am?!" I countered. Because, like I said, she was my brand-new mother-in-law. Standing there stunned, it was the only response I had. Plus, lines hadn't been drawn, and boundaries hadn't been set. Meanwhile, my brain was thinking, *Oh, hell no! SHE did NOT just say what I thought she said!*

I guess her ears also heard what she said, out loud, and she attempted to recover by saying, "You just look smaller with your clothes on." Like that was any better.

I thought that was the craziest thing anyone had ever said to me, to my face at least, and I burst out laughing. Yes, I cracked up and bellowed back, "Well, thank you very much! I'll have to remember that!"

That was the moment my relationship with my mother-in-law began. I was standing on her home turf, in a bikini. She was staring dead at my stomach. I was five-foot-one, weighed a hundred and seven pounds, and had been her daughter-in-law for an entire week. Grinning ear to ear, I thought to myself, *THIS is what I've been training for my whole life, lady. Bring it on.*

Two Things Can Be True at the Same Time

Billy Reid and I blended our families and married on June 24th in the year of our Lord, Sweet Baby Jesus, *what in the absolute hell have I gotten myself into*, 2000. And Martha Jean Robertson Reid became my mother-in-law. She was the youngest of four and the only girl. She had been a princess until the ripe age of seventeen, when she married Bill Reid, Billy Reid's father. Then she became the Queen. She became Mrs. Reid, which in the South, when you drawl it out like you have marbles in your mouth, sounds a lot like "misery." Go ahead, try it. Out loud. I'll wait.

It might take you a couple of times, but you'll get there. There it is! Did you hear it?

I christened her *Mother*. She loved the title. We both did. Her for the esteem associated with it, as if she'd somehow been elevated to Queen Mother Superior. And I for the slang interpretation, as she could be such a *mother*(bleeper)! You know how women tend to put their sons on a pedestal? Nope.

Not her. She didn't have one fiber of nurturing instinct in her entire being.

When she'd tell me stories of back in the day, I'd always inquire about where Billy Reid had been at the time, since her story would have made him no more than a young kid. Yes, I call him by his first and last name. I don't know why. Always have. Always do. I guess it just sounds right. Anyway, her nonchalant, slightly put-off response was always the same: "Lord, I don't know. I suppose he was with me or around somewhere." *Don't hold your breath for the Mother of the Year Award!*

I never had the pleasure of meeting my father-in-law, Bill Reid, whom I hear was the nurturer in the family. At least to his firstborn, Mary Delight Reid. Yes, her middle name is Delight because, as legend has it, her father took one look at her and was tickled to pieces, as revealed by the moniker he bestowed on her at birth. I suppose it could have been worse. Mary Tickled Reid doesn't land the same way. I'm telling you, this story writes itself. I highly doubt I'd have called him Father. I imagine I would have stuck with Bill Reid or maybe Saint Bill. Although Billy Reid would beg to differ, seeing as Mary Delight was the only apple of his father's eye.

Meanwhile, Billy Reid was always under his parents' watchful eyes, having worked for them his entire life. He was the third generation to work at his family's establishment, The Cupboard Restaurant, in

Charlotte, North Carolina. He never lived more than two miles away from his parents. He was constantly under their scrutiny. Even after he took over the business and ran it successfully on his own for many years, his mother kept a critical eye on him. When his expenses went up a dollar and he raised the prices a quarter, longtime customers would tattle on him to Queen Misery as if he'd tried to knock over a bank!

When I was nineteen years old, before I got married the first time, a man at the fair read my palm. He said that I would have four children, and the oldest would be twins. I always thought it would be so cool to have twins. Mothergrand (which is what I called my grandmother, at her request— come to think of it, I guess I've always been around women with illusions of grandeur) had sisters who were twins. Myrtle and Myrtis. Yep, and her name was Mildred. Thank the lawd, Fathergrand ... yes, Mothergrand's idea ... called her by her maiden name, Porter. Or should I say *Portah*, him being from Charleston, South Carolina, and Mothergrand hailing from Alabama!

At twenty-six years old, I gave birth to my son Porter. Just Porter. No other buns in the oven. I thought about what the carnival dude predicted and figured he was a sham. But, hey! I'd had at least five dollars' worth of fun imagining for several years that I was destined to have multiples. Even as a kid, I wanted twins. I loved the board game Life when I was little. I loved it when I landed on twins, *and* I got a career as an artist! That was the best!

So there I was, thirty-two years old, marrying Billy Reid, who was fourteen years my senior and had three boys of his own! (Did anyone else just read that and hear the Brady Bunch theme rise up in the background? Hello there, fellow latchkey kid!) Chris and Scott were eighteen years old, Alex was thirteen years old, and Porter was five years old when we got married. Yessiree, Bob! I have four children, and the oldest are twins! It made me realize that you end up where you're supposed to be, just not how you thought you'd get there.

The Cupboard was closed one week out of the year. One week. Period. The week of July 4th. And *that* is when we went on our honeymoon. If you can even call it that. Our honeymoon consisted of me, Billy Reid, our four kids, my sister-in-law, her husband, a nephew, and Mother, because it was Mother's beach house. That is how I found myself face-to-face with her, squaring off in a two-piece with the Queen of the Castle.

I subscribe to, and am fascinated by, the concept that two things can be true at the same time. Whenever asked about my relationship with Billy Reid's mom, I'd always reply, "Oh gawd! Billy Reid's mom is awful! She's such a bitch! My mother-in-law and I get along great, though!" It's absolutely bizarre! Having been a hairdresser for over thirty years, I always say I have my honorary PhD in human behavior. And I'll tell you what, Mother has been quite the case study!

She was one of the most self-absorbed, narcissistic, oblivious, entertaining characters I have ever met. She navigated relationships based on what people could do for her. If someone got in her viewfinder, they became her person until she tired of them and found someone else to do her bidding. I call it the "tastes like chicken" syndrome. She got bored, like when you've had chicken too many meals in a row and you're ready for something different. That is what energy vampires do! They move on to fresh meat.

She never said please. She never asked. She always, without fail, said, "I'm going to *let* you take me to the *doctah*" or "I'm going to *let* you bring me *suppah*." Those aren't typos. That's how she sounded. She spoke with a distinct Southern air, an arrogance almost. It was hilarious!

Now is probably as good a time as any for a vernacular lesson. In the South, true old Southerners have their own language of sorts that requires some interpretation. It's the verbal version of cursive, which apparently is becoming extinct as well! Here are a few pointers that may help:

Oftentimes, when a word has the letter *R* in it, it is pronounced *ah*. For example, she once had dogs named Butler and Scarlet. I know! I know! Of course she did! You can't make this stuff up! She called them *Butlah* and *Scaahlet!*

When referring to a grave subject matter, it is often necessary to add *The* to it, with a capital *T* for effect. As in *Mary had The Cansah*. That would be cancer. Or, in Mother's case, she would have said, "May-ree had The Cansah."

Sometimes things are singularized, as in *diabetes*. That would be referred to as *The Diabete*, or less formally, *The Sugar*. As in *Billy Reid needs to watch what he eats, or he's gonna get The Sugah.*

There is only one thing that is never singular. Grits! Those are always plural. Once at a restaurant in North Myrtle Beach, I found it necessary to enlighten a gentleman from Vermont. His breakfast came, and I overheard him ask his family if anyone wanted to try a grit. *A grit!* It was like nails on a chalkboard. Nothing in me could let this man go uninformed. Being of public service and all, I politely told him the error of his ways.

◉ ◉ ◉

I have never had a relationship with anyone like I had with The Queen Mother Misery. I love my own mom. I love me some Billy Reid. I love my children and grandchildren. I love my friends, family, clients, and neighbors. Yet there is something entirely different about my kinship with her. What started out as me being a buffer for my husband and his mother, in some weird way, turned into the most authentic, real, completely honest interaction I have ever had with anyone. I have never once worried about what she thought of me. Hell, if you're interacting with someone that frank, you don't have to wonder.

We were kindred spirits in that way. We were both straightforward, having little to no filter and thinking out loud more than I care to admit. For the nearly twenty-five-plus years I knew her, I showed up 100 percent myself. I came to cherish the true gift our relationship was to me, and I believe it was to her as well.

Now that doesn't imply I didn't want to wring her neck a time or two ... HUNDRED! It means that I mined some real gold from my moments with her, *and* some felt like actual mining! Not just a figure of speech!

As a hairdresser, I have entertained my clients for over two decades with stories about Mother. They've always thought her antics needed to be published. I have posted numerous pictures of our adventures together. She even has her own hashtag, #youcantshootyourmotherinlaw. You can look up our shenanigans on Instagram. She took it all in great fun.

This is my story of being Martha Reid's daughter-in-law, along with stories of other strong women, who were the training ground that readied me for all our relationship had to offer, even if I didn't realize it at the time. Sometimes it's a love story. Sometimes it's a story about tolerating. Sometimes it's a "you can't make this shit up" story.

Regardless, it's a story about being human and honoring that in others, even when we don't see eye-to-eye, be it politically, religiously, or in terms of lifestyle. That's the power of two things being true at the same time. We are all allowed to take up space and can navigate doing so with respect and humor.

May you get a kick out of her like I did. May you be left with levity to embrace your own prickly relationships with more ease. May you find your voice in your relationships, if that is the takeaway you need. May you, at the very least, find a refreshing escape, much like going to the beauty salon.

Wax On, Wax Off, Sister Miyagi

I've been fortunate enough to have always been surrounded by and supported by strong, capable women. Each one adding to my proverbial toolbox. Filling it with skills to navigate my life. Each one contributing to my soul with their own lessons learned, creating this crazy concoction of a lens through which I view the world around me. And unwittingly setting me up for my relationship with Mother.

When I was around three years old, my Aunt Susan came to live with us. By us, I mean my mom and me. Susan was the ripe old age of twenty, and my mom was twenty-two. It was a different time. Looking back, it seems that times were harder and easier. It's interesting how both of those statements can be true. Maybe what I mean is that times were simpler.

I remember gasoline being rationed in the 1970s, and there were only certain days of the week you could fill up. If your license tag ended in an odd number, you could go to the pumps on odd-numbered days. Even-numbered tags could go on the other days. I guess the odd-numbered tag owners felt like they'd won the lottery if a month wrapped up on the 31st and they were able to go back and top off on the 1st.

Nowadays, I guess people with vanity tags would assume they could go whenever they pleased. Can you imagine telling a bunch of pandemic toilet paper hoarders which day their tushies could go get gas? No pun intended!

We didn't live on a very savory side of town. My mom did the best she could, and Susan moving in certainly eased the situation. I'd see my father every once in a while when he needed a sofa to crash on. It was a very fluid, hippie-esque living situation. The spring before I was to start first grade, my mom and I attended an open house for prospective students at our neighborhood's assigned school. That place was a dump! I remember coming home, putting my tiny hands on my tiny hips while stomping my tiny feet, and announcing I would not be attending that school because it was dirty, and it smelled funny. I did not get a good vibe, and I was having none of it.

To this day, I think the meanest thing you can say about a person or a place is that they look like they smell bad!

My mom thought, *Well hell's bells! What am I supposed to do now?*

What she did was pack us up and move us to another neighborhood that was only slightly more desirable at the time. However, it was near St. Patrick Catholic School, and I don't recall getting a chance to preview the campus before starting my elementary school tenure there. Apparently, I wasn't the only one getting educated. Mom outsmarted me on this one.

I loved attending St. Pat's. It made so many lasting impressions on me. Many of which I'm sure were not part of the intended curriculum.

To this day, I still pray for the baby about to be born into the world every time I hear the scream of an ambulance siren. I acquired this habit while talking to a plant. More specifically, in second grade, I learned to pray for the unborn while caring for my bean plant that sprouted in a cup. We were doing a science experiment where we talked to our plants to see if they would grow faster. Something about how we expel carbon dioxide, which plants need, and they, in turn, produce oxygen, which we need.

I am quite the talker, so you know Jack himself would have been mad jealous about the size of my stalk.

Once, while standing by the windows where our plants were lined up, we could see first responders racing by our school with lights flashing and sirens blaring. It was quite unnerving for a bunch of seven- and eight-year-olds. Sister Elizabeth could see our concern and assured us that there was nothing to worry about. It was just a mom being transported to the hospital to have her baby, and we should take a second to offer up a prayer for them. As far as praying for the new babies, St. Pat's is spitting distance from the hospital, so I got lots of prayer practice.

Now I know that the process of talking to plants to help them grow is called the "carbon dioxide fertilization effect." And regarding the sirens, I realize that it's probably a couple of EMTs careening toward the ER, hauling some old dude having the mother of all widow-maker heart attacks, or some guy who ate asphalt while riding his motorcycle.

Second grade is also the time when you prepare for your first penance, or confession, and your first communion. In the Catholic faith, you cleanse your sins to make way for receiving the Eucharist, or the body of Christ, through confession. Here's how that experience played out for me.

The first time I was to confess my sins, it seemed like any other normal conversation with a grown-up. There was no confessional with a screen between us. Just two people sitting face-to-face on folding metal chairs. One had spent a large portion of their life pondering the Mysteries of the Universe, and the other one was a priest. At eight years old, I was preoccupied with getting to the bottom of things.

I remember Father What's-His-Face (because I don't recall his actual name) telling me that from now on, I would have a direct link to God through him. I also remember telling him that I didn't think that sounded like a direct link. I didn't understand why I couldn't just talk to God myself, like I'd been doing all along. I don't recall his reaction, but I'm pretty sure he wrapped it up by assigning me several Our Fathers and a few Hail Marys for good measure!

Thanks to Sister Carolyn, third grade was when my singing career ended before it ever had a chance to take off. One day, while teaching us hymns in religion class, Sister Carolyn became distraught over some awful sound she was being subjected to. I thought she must have amazing hearing, kind of like how only dogs can detect those high-pitched whistles, because I didn't notice anything out of the ordinary, certainly nothing worthy of throwing her hands in the air and demanding that we all stop at once!

Determined to find the culprit, she proceeded to pace back and forth while we were singing, coming to land right in front of me. She demanded that I and the two students to my left take it from the top. Next, she had me and my two classmates to my right try it again. Then she asked me and the person on each side of me to give it a go one more time. Ahhh. I can still remember the relief in her eyes when she figured it out.

It was me! I was the one, or should I say my singing voice was the one, that sounded like nails on a chalkboard for her. She decided that the best contribution I could make to the choir was to simply mouth the words to the song, and she didn't hesitate to tell me so. In front of my entire class! So much for singing a joyful noise unto the Lord. Jeez!

⊙ ⊙ ⊙

Under the umbrella of you-can't-make-this-stuff-up, I found myself sitting in a pew behind Sister Carolyn recently. My sweet friend Colleen had passed away, and I attended her funeral. She grew up in Charlotte, attended Catholic school, raised her family in the community, and worked as a nurse for many years. I was blown away by how many people filed into the funeral home. By my count, four generations were there to bid her farewell. To say she was loved doesn't even begin to describe the energy in the room. Although I was thirty minutes early, which is a miracle in and of itself, people from every phase of her abundant life were already packed in like sardines and spilling out into the parking lot.

I scanned the room for a place to stand and saw my best friend, Shelly, and her husband, Cole, waving me over. I gratefully squeezed in between them. I offered to switch seats so they could sit next to each other. Giving me one of the greatest compliments I could receive, Cole said, "Sitting next to you is like sitting next to Shelly. Y'all are practically the same person." He's not wrong. I don't think we've ever gone anywhere and not been mistaken for sisters.

Speaking of sisters! At that moment, Shelly brought to my attention that we were sitting behind a row of nuns! I had attended St. Patrick's until the eighth grade, when my family moved to Mississippi, ending my Catholic tenure. Shelly and I had become each other's person when her family moved to Charlotte in the fifth grade. Having gone on to graduate from Charlotte Catholic High School, she knew many people whom I did not.

Before the service started, she asked me if I recognized anyone. She pointed to a woman sitting diagonally in front of us and whispered, "Do you remember Sister Carolyn?" I replied, "Are you kidding me?! Do I remember her? I just wrote an essay about how she ended my singing career before it started!" Shelly asked me what happened, and I recounted the story to her. She laughed and said, "The same thing happened to me in high school, but it was by that woman." She pointed to a woman who was sitting diagonally in front of us in the opposite direction! We got the giggles and decided we are even more alike than we thought!

We must have caught Sister Carolyn's attention, because it was right about then that she looked over her shoulder and recognized Shelly. Shelly asked her if she remembered me from St. Pat's, even conjuring up my maiden name. It was clear that Sister Carolyn had no recollection of me or the havoc I'd played on her auditory system. Isn't it amazing how what can be a defining moment in one person's life doesn't even register as a blip on the radar screen for someone else? Either way, Shelly and I weren't taking any chances! When it came time to sing, we shook our heads at each other like there was no way in hell those two ladies would ever hear a peep out of us again.

◉ ◉ ◉

Back to third grade, Sister Julia was also caught off guard. That nun was a throwback, an old-school sister. She was mean. I'd heard stories of the nuns my parents, aunts, and uncles were taught by, who used rulers to crack knuckles and paddles to pop behinds. Sister Julia seemed like she would have enjoyed teaching them.

I still remember the fluster on her face when our class returned to school one Monday to an entire cage filled with gerbils, where there had only been a couple when we'd left the previous Friday. We all had so many questions, and she didn't have an answer to any of them. I, myself, knew a little about "the birds and the bees," so I figured it translated to gerbils too. Things like one of the gerbils had to be the daddy, and the other one was the mommy. And that the babies popped right out through the mommy's belly button. My mom told me that babies pop right out. I figured out the belly button part on my own.

Around that same time, a new restaurant opened up around the corner from our house. Art's BBQ. Mom promised we would get takeout from there one night. I was definitely the kind of kid you didn't tell something to unless you meant it, because I would hold you to it. The day came, and I was so excited. The only time I ever got to eat at a restaurant was when my father (aka Daddio) would show up a few times a year to take me to Shoney's to celebrate my report card.

I kept interrupting and asking when we would get dinner. I'm not sure how many "in a minute" hours passed by when I decided to take matters into my own hands. I grabbed some cash out of my mom's purse, walked around the corner to Art's, ordered three dinners, and returned home without them ever realizing I'd gone anywhere in the first place.

Living with my mom and aunt was like having roommates. We'd get home from work and school, and we would chit-chat around the kitchen table for hours on end. I'd sit and do my homework while we all recounted our days to each other. Thank goodness they'd occasionally double-check my assignments, like the time they realized with all of the conversations and the stops and starts to help me, they had inadvertently told me to spell butterflies as B-U-T-T-F-U-T-T-E-R-S. That would have gone over really well with ole Sister Mean Jeans!

During our time there we also had the most amazing slumber parties in the kitchen. They were the best! We would scoot the table and chairs over to make way for our mattresses. We'd spend the entire night baking cookies and lounging around playing games. It was a blast!

In actuality, we had oil heat and could only afford to have it delivered once a month. When it was gone, it was gone. When it was particularly cold out and the month lasted more than twenty-nine to thirty days, it would always run out. Every month, I would pray that we'd run out of oil so we could do the slumber party again. It all seemed simple enough to me. No oil equaled tons of fun! From a young age, I somehow figured out how to make the most of any situation and to take matters into my own hands when I could. Seems like resilience is hardwired into my DNA.

Puff, Puff, Pass

Being the oldest of ten, my mom has a knack for seeing what needs to happen to keep things from going off the rails. She has an unusual ability to see the big picture *and* the smallest details. Her philosophy on parenting has definitely formed who I've become. Her tenets are to raise your children to think for themselves and to let them know they are loved. She's a very decisive person. She's taught me not to waffle. To make a decision and see how it goes. Trusting I can make another decision down the road and incrementally tweak my path as I go. Understanding that *not* making a decision *is* making a decision, and that I concede my power in not doing so. In short, she just handles shit, remaining calm in the midst of it all.

Once, when I was around five years old, I came home from spending the weekend at Daddio's house. I recounted our escapades to my mom and Aunt Susan, who still lived with us. "Oh, we had so much fun!" I told them. I went on to explain that Daddio had taken an empty yellow plastic Parkay margarine container and fashioned the lid into the face of a clock, using a thumbtack and construction paper for the hands to maneuver. He sat cross-legged and leaned against his sofa. I sat with my rear end on the floor, my back against his chest, and my legs slung over his feet while mine dangled in midair. We sat like that til both our legs, or should I say all four of our legs, were asleep, and I knew how to tell time. We'd eaten peanut butter and marshmallow fluff sandwiches, basic nectar-of-the-gods cuisine. And the best part! Several of his friends came over and sat on the floor in a circle. I got to stand in the middle and ever so carefully go from one friend to the next, handing them this beautiful, ornate, feathery thing, making sure not to touch the end so I didn't get burned.

My mom and Susan listened intently, smiling with each detail. My mom politely excused herself, telling us that she needed to phone my father real quick, as she had forgotten to tell him something. Not making a big deal about it, she left the room to make the call. I couldn't hear their conversation, which I'm sure included reaming him a new asshole! She didn't blame, shame, or explain. She just handled it. I continued to see my father, and his friends would still come by. It just no longer involved me passing a roach clip. She nipped it in the bud, so to speak.

I grew up in a household where we talked about everything. No subject felt taboo. I am definitely comfortable communicating. In fact, I think communication is greatly misunderstood. For years, as a salon owner, I would tell my team and our clients, "I can't fix what I don't know. You have to tell me what's going on, what you're feeling, and what you're thinking." I was almost always met with "I'm not comfortable with confrontation," usually with an added "like you are!"

I would always explain that I'm not confrontational, although I can be. However, asking what the problem is, willingly listening so all involved feel heard, creating suggestions, and giving options for resolution is not confrontation. It's communication. Confrontation is when communication has repeatedly not occurred, and feelings have been stuffed down. Add in some resentment over real or misconstrued events, and you've got yourself a situation ripe for confrontation. A volcano, as we say in the South, fixin' to blow! People often don't want to communicate for fear of hurting someone's feelings. Have you ever had a bottled-up spew of grievances directed at you? Talk about pain!

My mom's resolve taught me not to be afraid to go toe-to-toe with people, even in difficult situations. This helped bring me one step closer to being prepared for Mother.

Now I Get It

I got married for the first time at the age of twenty-one. My first mother-in-law was not my fan, and she wasn't shy in letting me know. She didn't come right out and say it, at least not to me. She didn't have to; I could feel it in our interactions. Although she didn't hesitate to let her son know. I can still see him standing before me, distraught, having just gotten into a huge fight with his mother. He was shaking as he shared what his mom said about me. She told him that I cussed and didn't wear a bra!

I smile thinking about that now. It's been nearly forty years. Of course, it stung at the time! She was right. I did cuss. I still do. And worse! *And* I didn't wear a bra. I didn't have anything to put in one! Oh, how I miss *those days!* We were so young! I don't miss my youth as much as I miss not wearing a bra.

She was right in so many ways, so many intangible ways. She stated the obvious. Her family *had* been invaded by a braless sailor mouth! What she didn't have the point of reference for was that her family dynamic was changing. What I think, looking back now, is that she innately knew I wasn't right for her son or her family. Her mother's intuition instantly knew what took me eight years to realize.

She was strong-willed and told it like it was. A force to be reckoned with. Her sheer presence and her laugh could fill up a room. She had a handshake so firm I saw it bring a wince to most. My father, caught off guard by their introduction, referred to her as a doberman with earrings! I never understood her intensity or the way she navigated through the world. Until I did. It took a little history lesson. One I stumbled upon.

Fifteen years after my divorce, the Levine Museum of the New South had an exhibit called *Purses, Platforms & Power: Women Changing Charlotte in the 1970s*. My salon, T. Reid and Company, was a corporate sponsor for a grand opening event and fashion show. Before the event, I was able to explore the exhibit and take my time without the throngs of attendees. It was incredibly powerful.

The entrance to the exhibit had two doors. One was marked "Doctor," "Lawyer," "Judge," "Politician," "CEO," and the like. The other door said "Homemaker," "Teacher," "Nurse," and "Secretary," and that was about it. Visitors got to choose which door they would like to enter the exhibit through. That's when people realized only one door was unlocked. Only one door granted access. Yep, the homemaker, teacher, nurse, secretary option. The other door didn't budge.

Once inside, everything was in black and white. There were artifacts and timelines of the Women's Suffrage Movement, of women demanding the right to vote. Displays from local universities, which were once women's colleges where women were able to join the workforce in nursing and teaching. Old photographs of classrooms and hospitals. Not to minimize the fact that women can now vote, the beginning of the exhibit was pretty tame. Important, but lackluster.

Right when you're thinking, *Is this it?* Bam! You turn the corner, and a sign announces, "Then the 1970s came, and everything changed!" Access was granted to the next phase by walking through a doorway with groovy beaded strands hanging and playfully inviting you in. It was *amazing!* So vibrant and full of life. Shades of yellow, orange, and avocado exploded! There was so much going on that it was almost overwhelming.

I could feel the shift in energy. I, of course, had been alive during that time, but I had experienced it from a child's perspective. Now, as a grown woman, a mother, a wife, and a business owner who was about to emcee the grand opening event for this exhibit, to say that this room landed with an impact would be an understatement. I was standing there, taking it all in, scanning the room, looking for a place to get my bearings.

That was when I saw her! My first mother-in-law! On display! A part of history! She was one of the first two women to anchor the local evening news. It all came together for me at that moment. I call those Tetris moments. Something clicked, and all of those seemingly random pieces fit together. The pattern appeared. I got it.

Unfortunately, as is sometimes the case, when I had been part of her family, we were often desensitized to her recounts of past accomplishments. We heard her stories, repeatedly, not really understanding the impact she'd made or the trails she'd blazed.

Without meaning to be, we are often dismissive of the ones we are the closest to, making it hard for them to be prophets in their own land. We just see them in the relationship we have with them and don't consider them in any other context.

Standing there, seeing her in a museum exhibit, I realized she had arm-wrestled the way for the rest of us. She'd navigated the times the way she needed to, and by doing so, had created a space that allowed me to be the way I am. She got the world ready for the likes of me, even if she wasn't ready for me. And she most definitely prepared me for my future mother-in-law! I am eternally grateful, and I never got the opportunity to properly thank her. She passed away the week I was inspired to write this very story about her, and it gives me great peace that she is once again paving the way. Most likely giving heaven some hell! And it will be better for it.

A Tale of Two Helens

Since becoming part of the Reid clan, every time we are at the beach, we eat at a family-run country-cooking place called Hoskins. They've been in business since 1948. It's what's known around here as a "meat 'n' three." Meaning they have a daily lunch special of various protein and vegetable options. And yes, mac and cheese is a veggie option, just like rice and gravy. Y'all didn't know this doubles as a reference book of sorts, did ya?

There's an art to ordering at Hoskins. To make the process faster for the waitress and the kitchen, you order the meat you *do* want of the three or four daily choices and the side you *don't* want of those four options. It somehow magically translates into getting exactly what you want! I think it's the only place in the universe where you get what you desire by speaking into existence what you don't desire! It goes against what I've learned about the Law of Attraction over the last four decades. I guess there *is* an exception to every rule.

There's always a line out the door and down the sidewalk. You just file in at the end, and someone periodically comes out with a scratchpad, asks how many are in your party, and if everyone is there yet. No reservations. No call-ahead seating. No putting your name in at a hostess stand. They serve breakfast, lunch, and dinner. They're closed around Thanksgiving until when they damn well please, starting sometime in early February, usually before Valentine's Day.

When Hoskins reopens for the season, there's no signage or fanfare. There's something intrinsic about it. It's the closest thing I've ever seen to humans having a collective, internal, unspoken dispersion and reassembly. It's akin to a salmon run, or a whale migration, or witnessing geese fly south for the winter, returning when conditions are ripe. You just instinctively know when to quit going and when to show back up. Everyone is slimmer or more expanded, be it at the waistline or family additions. A little taller or more stooped than the last time. A little more gray here and there.

The constant at Hoskins is Helen. Mean-Ass Helen. For years, there were two Helens. Sweet, white-haired Helen and spitfire, red-headed Helen. Billy Reid and I nicknamed her Mean-Ass Helen. She, as they say, doesn't give one single fuck. She loves her regulars, and she'll get to the rest of you folks when she gets around to it. *If* she gets around to it. It doesn't matter if your tea glass has dried up like the Sahara Desert and the cornbread crumbs collected in your throat have you gasping for your last breath. If she's in the middle of one of her tales at a neighboring table, you'd best conserve your resources and figure out how not to freak all the way out 'til she gets around to you for a refill.

Daddio used to say that you get what you resist, and Mean-Ass Helen was the teacher who drove that lesson home for me. One summer, Billy Reid and I got seated in her section every damn time! She was the worst! We got to the point that when it was our turn, we would ask who was going to be our server. If it was Ms. Mean-Ass, we'd decide if we wanted to bake on the sidewalk a while longer, waiting for another table to open up.

One day, I turned to Billy Reid and said, "This is ridiculous! We are going to embrace this woman. We are going to start requesting her section, even if it means we have to wait in line forever. She is either going to love us, or we're going to die of thirst. Whatever happens, we are done resisting this situation." Plus, we had enough going on with Mother that we didn't need to let Mean-Ass Helen get under our skin.

Guess what happened? We fell in love with Mean-Ass Helen! And it's mutual. She's still as snarky as she ever was. She loves to tell people about how she wore us down, usually while newcomers are eyeing her to come take their order already! She enjoys telling customers about our adventures together, like the time we took her and her late husband, Hilton, to Ruth's Chris Steak House. Hilton slid over to let the valet attendant hop in the car because he thought we knew the guy and he was catching a ride with us. He'd never seen such a big to-do. Or the time after Hilton passed away that we took her to Flamingo Grill, a Myrtle Beach time capsule of a treasure. That's where Helen was introduced to moscow mules that went down smooth. She and I piled up in the back seat afterward, and she commanded Billy Reid, who doesn't drink and good-naturedly tolerates our nonsense, "On, James! Chauffeur us home!"

Helen is unapologetically herself. Always, in all ways. I've seen her make men half her age blush. She captivates her audience, amusing them with her collection of stories from her history of bad decisions. She says things like, "Sugar, beauty is only a light switch away." And one of my personal favorites, "If I can't have fun, I'll just stay to the porch at home."

I'm so grateful that we didn't just write her off as a heiny biddy. In all these years, she hasn't changed one iota. *We* did—or at least, our approach did. And thank goodness, because we would have missed out on the joy and friendship she has brought to our lives. Last I checked, the other Helen, who retired eons ago, is no longer with us. RIP, Sweet Helen. Billy Joel wasn't wrong when he sang, "Only the Good Die Young." I suspect Mean-Ass and I will be hanging out for years to come. At least, I plan on it.

The Bigger the Hair, The Smaller the Butt

Mother always loved coming to my salon, T. Reid and Company. Everyone, clients and team members alike, called her Mother, just like I did. Someone from the desk would be on the lookout around her appointment time to help her get in and settled. At that point, she'd *let* me make her coffee. She loved the way I made it the best because I put way too much cream and sugar in it. She liked to pretend that she would never add that much stuff! *Whatever, Mother. Just say thank you.*

Years ago, Mother and my sister-in-law, Mary, came in together to get their hair done. Mother wanted a roller set, so I had her wound tighter than a top and under the dryer set to cremate—because, in her words, "Oh, that heat feels so good!" and one can only hope. I was finishing up Mary's hair, and she stood up to get a closer look in the mirror at her new 'do.

Mother, who had no concept of how loudly she was talking because her hood dryer was on full blast, proceeded to yell at the top of her lungs in a crowded salon, "MAY-REE, I BELIEVE YOUR BUTT IS THE SMALLEST IT'S BEEN IN A LONG TIME!"

The entire salon exploded with laughter. I turned to my sister-in-law, who was clearly seeing some results with Weight Watchers, and said, "Mary, I think that was a compliment." She replied, "Oh, it was. She's been my momma for a looooong time. Trust me, *that* was a compliment."

On another one of Mother's "trips to the shop," as she liked to call it, she brought her dog Millie along for the ride. Millie stayed in the car while Mother got her hair done. Yes, don't worry, the windows were cracked. Yes, it was nice and pleasant outside. Mother liked dogs more than people, and Millie was her heart, so her furbaby was perfectly safe.

One of my stylists, Noel, had the great pleasure of escorting Mother to her car that day. I'm sure she grabbed him with that bony death grip of hers as he was racing by to collect his next client, and announced that she was going to *let* him walk her to her car. He was a good sport about it and genuinely found her entertaining, so he was game. As they opened the car door, Mother discovered Millie had thrown up on the seat. Again, animal lovers and activists alike, I can assure you that Millie was under no duress. She loved tagging along.

Mother turned to Noel and said, "Be a dea-yah and get something to wipe that up." Noel hauled ass back inside, grabbing wet paper towels and a dry hand towel. He proceeded to wipe up Millie's puke with the dry hand towel, then gave the seat a once-over with the wet paper towels. Mother didn't say, "Thank you. Wow, that's great. I'm so happy I didn't have to deal with that." Nope. She said, "*I* would have taken the wet papah towels and picked it up. *Then* I would have wiped the seat off with the dry towel." She fished a whopping seventy-three cents, mostly in pennies, out of her ashtray for his trouble.

About three years later, I was driving Mother and Millie home from the beach. We got approximately two miles from her house, and the damn dog threw up in the car. Mother didn't skip a beat. She leaned over the armrest between us, looked at me mischievously, and said, "You don't suppose Noel is at the shop. We could swing by, and he can clean that up for us."

Spoken like a true queen.

Plain Ole Gay

Billy Reid grew up going to North Myrtle Beach, South Carolina. Living in Charlotte, North Carolina, it's an easy weekend getaway. Mother was always very generous about letting us use her beach house whenever we found the time to go. There was the cutest little row of four townhomes diagonally across the street from her home, which was one block closer to the ocean. For years and years, as Billy Reid and I hauled our stuff past it on the way to the beach, we would dream out loud about how we wanted to buy the one on the end if it ever became available.

One day, our friend Renda, who owned a unit on the other end, called to let us know that the owners of the spot we wanted were ready to sell. We were so excited! Once conversations were had and negotiations were met, we agreed to buy it. The only thing left to do before closing was to let Mother know we would be her neighbors.

I called to tell her that we would be coming by shortly and that we had some news to share. She could not hear for shit, so I wasn't going to scream our plans to her over the phone. To alleviate any concern she may have had about our impending conversation, I told her nothing was wrong, and we weren't coming to ask her for money.

Isn't that pretty much all you need to know if someone calls to say that they are coming to talk to you about something? Plus, my sister-in-law, Mary, was always calling her with some drama that required a handout. So off we went to tell her what we were up to.

Mother immediately planted a seed of doubt in my husband by saying, "Billy, are you sure? You know I'm planning on leaving you my beach house someday."

This was actual news to us, so I asked, "Great! When's that?"

To which she replied, "When I die."

I countered, "Even better! When's that?" And added, "Why don't you let us go ahead and buy your place instead?"

"NOPE!" she said. "I want to own EVERYTHING 'til the day I die!"

After a lot of back and forth about someday this and someday that, and how we couldn't do this, and make sure you never do that, and you can never get rid of anything in it, we bought our own place. Our own glorious place!

The first time we drove Mother down after we bought our little beach haven, she walked in and announced, "I want to trade! Your place is cute-ah than mine!"

I responded, "Oh, hell no! You missed your chance, Sister!"

As beach neighbors, we began a morning ritual of sharing coffee and the paper, clad in our pajamas in Mother's backyard. One morning, I found her trying to make sense of the latest headlines she was reading, specifically, North Carolina's Bathroom Bill, or HB2, and something called "transgender." It was regarding Caitlyn Jenner (formerly known as Bruce Jenner), a gold medalist in what some may consider the biggest physical test of manhood, the Olympic decathlon. To say that she was all kindsa confused would be an understatement.

I started explaining to her that HB2 meant a person had to use the bathroom facilities based on the parts they were born with, not on the gender they identify with. I told her, yes, we looked like a "buncha yayhoos" to the rest of the country. I went on to spell out as succinctly as possible to my eighty-five-year-old mother-in-law that transgender means that you might look like one gender on the outside, but you feel like a completely different gender on the inside.

During this discussion, I got a phone call from my salon. Mitch, a man who had been working the front desk while he was finishing up his degree in marketing, was calling to let me know that he had found "a real job" and was giving me his two weeks' notice. I loved it when people left my company to go get a *real job*. I guess I should have stopped paying them in Monopoly money! Just kidding! I knew Mitch's stint at the salon was short-lived, and he, of course, had my blessing to go. When I hung up, Mother wanted to know about my phone call. Now, keep in mind, Mother adored Mitch, AND she was chock-full of new knowledge from that morning's current events lesson.

She inquired, "Is Mitch one of *those*?"

I replied, "By one of *those*, do you mean transgender?"

She responded, "Yes, transgendah."

I said, "No, ma'am. Mitch is a gay man who likes men. He was born male, identifies as male, and goes potty in the men's room."

Mother thought about it for a moment, letting it all sink in, and asked, "So Mitch is just plain ole gay?"

I confirmed, "Yes, ma'am. Mitch is just plain-ole-garden-variety-everyday-run-of-the-mill gay."

She said, "Hmmmm." And that was that. She had it all sorted out.

I thought to myself, *That really is something. I don't know about Mitch's journey of self-realization, but I do know he is from a generation that typically didn't come out until well into adulthood. We've come a long way, baby, when a woman from the Depression era refers to someone as just "plain ole gay."*

Coveting Your Own Things

Mother absolutely adored acquiring things. One time, on the way to the beach, we passed a swing in a yard. She turned to me and said, "I want a swing like that. There are so many things I want. I also want a chiminea that I saw in the papah for a hundred dollahs at the Walmaht."

Here's the thing about Mother wanting shit. It was great and all, but you had to cart her slow, bony ass to collect those things. Which I would not have minded doing, except there was a catch. I learned pretty quickly that shopping was a sport for her, and once she'd obtained the once-sought-after object, she lost all interest. She was thrilled on the way home, and about a week later, she'd *let* you take it back for her. She once made me go to Belk, our regional department store, to return a bra that had been purchased three years earlier. It still had the tags on it. Curiously, Belk had tightened their return policy. Hmmm. Just sayin'. Coincidence? I think not.

When our twins, Chris and Scott, had their first apartment, Billy Reid and I staged our own *While You Were Out* makeover. Remember that TLC show where recipients would return home to a surprise makeover? It was Christmas Eve, and both boys worked in restaurants, so it was easy to be sneaky. Armed with a couple gallons of paint and a bazillion (that is NOT an exaggeration) jumbo lawn and leaf trash bags, we, along with a delivery of Ashley Furniture, transformed their shithole apartment into a thing of wonder.

◉ ◉ ◉

Sidenote: They both ended up courting their now wives there, so you can surmise that Billy Reid and I know a thing or two about putting lipstick on a pig. Translation: That's Southern for makin' sumthin' outta nuthin'.

◉ ◉ ◉

While doing so, we unearthed a sofa with great bones hidden under a slipcover. It was the only thing in the room that didn't make its way to the curb and instead, made its way to my salon. The boys obtained it via their cousin Beau, who'd received it years earlier from Mother. She let *nothing* go, so you can imagine how undesirable it looked after decades!

At the time, I was going through a phase where I would visit my interior designer friend Beth and rummage around the remnant room at her design firm. (Shout out to Lucy and Company! She always has *the most* divine fabrics!) There would be a yard of this, two of that, long strips of these three things, and a weird, mishmash assortment of material that I would take off her hands. I would barter these treasures for her next hairdo and spa treatment.

Next, I would head over to trade with my girlfriend Sabrina, who owns *the best* upholstery shop. (Shout out, Design Services of Charlotte! *That* is where the magic took place.) One day, I showed up with this bachelor pad sofa twice removed and proceeded to map out fourteen different materials on it to create a masterpiece.

My crowning upholstery achievement found its way to my salon waiting room, just in time for Mother to come waltzing in. She stopped dead—regrettably, merely a figure of speech—in her tracks and let out a "Wheyahhh"—that's *where;* Mother could soften an *R* in a word like it was a piece of taffy she'd been jawing on for a while—"did you get THAT?"

I explained, "This is the sofa you didn't want that you gave to Beau. When he didn't want it anymore, he gave it to the boys. When they were done with it, I took it to be reupholstered."

She declared, "WELL, I WANT IT BACK!" And that was that about that. Billy Reid came to collect it the next week, and it went right back into her living room, where she thoroughly enjoyed showing it off.

Coveting Other People's Things

Often on Sundays, Billy Reid would make a huge midday meal, and I would go pick up Mother to eat with us. She would plop her butt down at the table and *let* me fix her plate. Our wiener dogs, Dapple and Myers, would make a beeline to post up under her seat. They knew, between what she dropped accidentally and accidentally on purpose, that it was time to feast.

She was always cold at our house and would inevitably end up in one of my comfy sweaters or fluffy throws. Almost without fail, she would ask me if it was new or where I got it. I would think, O*kay, here it comes.*

She would casually begin, "I sure do wish I had a sweatah like this." Or something along the lines of, "I really do like this blanket. It's so pretty and soft."

I would respond, "Mother, would you like to take that home with you?"

"Oh, really?" she would exclaim. "I can have it?" She was like a little kid.

It's weird that in the nearly thirty years of knowing her, she only had us over to her house twice for a meal. The first was a birthday lunch for her best friend, Becky. (Becky, Becky, Becky. *There's* a story in and of itself.) Becky had been married to Eddie, my father-in-law's best friend. I never had the opportunity to meet Eddie or my father-in-law, Bill Reid. While married to Eddie, Becky worked as a nurse at a manufacturing plant. A man named Joe was an executive at the manufacturing plant. Becky and Joe fell in love. Eddie thought it was bullshit, was having none of it, and rode off on his motorcycle one day with what he could carry—which was nothing— leaving them to it.

Joe had kids from a previous marriage, and Becky had none. Becky and Joe proceeded to get married and adopt a little terrier-mix puppy. They named her Joy Delight. Yes, they borrowed my sister-in-law's middle name! I'm telling you. You can't make this up. It's pure gold. They dressed Joy Delight in her Sunday best every day, dresses complete with crinoline petticoats and matching headbands. She had quite the wardrobe. Fully grown, she was a size 4T, as in toddler. Every so often, Becky would revamp Joy Delight's wardrobe and take her gently used outfits to a high-end children's consignment shop at the beach. I say gently used because Joy Delight also spent the vast majority of her pampered existence being maneuvered around in a baby stroller.

Come to think of it, I don't know that I ever saw her paws touch the ground. Joy Delight even learned to brush her own teeth! With an actual toothbrush! Now *that* I have witnessed! Every year, Becky sent us a Christmas card with a picture of Joy Delight on Santa's lap. Joy Delight lived to be twenty years old. She had an obituary printed in the paper, and a local news station ran a story interviewing Becky. Mother complained to me about all of it. Between us, I think Mother was a little jealous of all the attention Becky was getting.

It didn't take long for Jill Delight, Joy Delight 2.0, to come onto the scene. She was the exact same breed, yet she was already full-grown. She appeared, to me, to be about a size 5T, the way she was squeezed into her hand-me-downs. The first time I met her, she was peering out from her stroller, headband cockeyed in front of her ears, and she had this wistful look in her eyes that said, "These people are nice and all, and it's great I was adopted and all, and I am cared for beyond belief and all, but can anyone please tell me what the actual hell is going on!?"

Okay, where was I? Oh yeah, the second time Mother had us over for a meal was about fifteen years after Becky's birthday luncheon. One Saturday morning, Billy Reid told me to call Mother and see if she'd like us to pick her up on our way to the farmer's market. I did a double-take to make sure he was okay. He would drop everything to help her with anything when she asked, yet he never willingly initiated spending time with her, nor she with him.

Off we went. Mother had a big time picking out a vast array of produce. We made a day of it. We took her to lunch and to run all our errands, dropping her off at home in the late afternoon. She called us a couple of hours later to see if we'd like to come over because she wanted to cook all of the vegetables she'd purchased. I'm not sure what the moon was doing or where all the planets were aligned, but Billy Reid accepted the invitation without hesitation. When we got to her house, Mother had not cooked one damn thing. She hadn't even removed anything from their containers.

I said, "Hey, lady! I thought you invited us over for dinner."

She came back with, "I know I invited you, but I didn't think you were going to say YES!" She clearly coveted our cooking over hers.

So Billy Reid and I proceeded to make dinner at the queen's house, while she proceeded to make herself comfortable.

Hold the Wambulance, We're Going to Walmart

Mother had moaning and groaning about her ailments down to a science. She reminded me of the Mrs. Beasley pull-string doll I had as a kid in the 1970s. You know, one of those Chatty Cathy-type dolls that say the same five phrases over and over again. Just keep pulling the string! She could go on forever about her complaints, stuck on a loop.

Remember the kids' song "Heads, Shoulders, Knees, and Toes"? Mother had her own rendition, and it went more like: "My glasses stay dirty, and I don't particularly care for my new ones, so I wear my old ones; I think I need hearing aids; my dentures aren't right, and I need to go to the periodontist; my shoulders are killing me, especially this right one; I need to poop because I haven't had a good poop today; my hips hurt so bad, it must be arthritis; I can barely get around; look how terrible my veins look; they absolutely throb at night and keep me up; my feet, oh my feet, I can't even begin to tell you how bad my feet are!"

Her invisible, internal pull string had to be the length of a football field! Every thirty seconds, she'd start the inventory scan of her bodily ailments and functions, reporting back in real time. Only one thing could distract her from her self-absorbed news bulletin: going to Walmart!

Oh, how Mother loved going to Walmart! And don't think for one second that the tires on the car made a single revolution without her being Ms. Bossy Britches from the passenger seat. She had something to say about every possible turn taken, from her driveway to the parking lot. We'd pull into a handicapped parking space of her choosing. I'd have to rummage through the treasure trove of a car door pocket filled with expired coupons, maps, umbrellas, and other assorted prizes to fish out the physician-issued handicap placard to hang just so. "No, not that way, the other way!" she'd say.

Please just get your ass out of the car, Mother!

And get, she did! That hobbly, wobbly, osteoporosis-riddled, self-proclaimed incapacitated octogenarian would find a shopping cart and BAM! She turned into the Flash! I, for the life of me, could not keep up with her. I'd follow behind her to the end of an aisle and blink—she would be gone! Vanished into thin air!

She was the type who would stand and read magazines cover to cover so that she didn't have to buy them. She once called me from the beach (and interrupted me with a client) to let me know that she had broken her personal record for time spent at a Walmart in a single visit. Five hours! She was tickled to pieces with herself. You'd have thought she was recounting a visit to Disney World, or the Vatican, or the Louvre.

The only other place that even came close to Walmart was Costco. Why? Samples. Yep, free samples. She would wander the aisles and "eat lunch." If the pickins were slim, there was always the lunch counter. She would get the "dollah fifty hot dog and soda combo."

Mercy me, folks, life just doesn't get much better!

Can't Get Anything
Over on You, Mother

When Mother turned seventy-eight, I decided to
throw her a surprise birthday party. Her birthday
fell on a Sunday, so that was easy enough. I invited
her over for Sunday lunch, per usual, raising no
suspicions. My big round table, which seats eight
comfortably, was packed with ten. The more, the
merrier. I simply adore a round dining room table!
You get to see everyone, hear everyone, and engage
with everyone. It doesn't matter who you get stuck
next to. Friends and family were waiting to greet her.
She had a big time. Queen for the day, holding court
with her people. She was so surprised! She even *let*
me make her plate. Lucky me!

Speaking of another kind of court, Mother knew
everything going on in college basketball. She knew
the teams, the players, the coaches, the rankings, and
the stats. She loved collegiate ball. She couldn't have
cared less about professional ball, *except* for LeBron
James. I have no earthly idea what her deal was, but
she loved him. I mean, besides the obvious that he's

amazing. She *let* me take her to see him when he was with the Cleveland Cavaliers, and they played the Charlotte Hornets. She had a big time cheering him on, not caring one single bit that she was rooting for the opposing team on home turf, her home turf, where she was born and raised.

Another time, Mother read in the newspaper that *Dixie's Tupperware Party* was coming to Charlotte. And guess what? Yep! She was going to *let* me escort her. So off we went to the Booth Playhouse at the Blumenthal Arts Center in Uptown Charlotte. Mother loved nothing better than to-go containers. *Can you even have enough?*

We were greeted by Miss Dixie herself, in the flesh, Adam's apple and all. There she stood at the door of the theater, Tupperware catalogs in hand, greeting each patron as if we were guests in her home. Mother was mesmerized and totally fangirling out, exclaiming, "Well, aren't you beautiful!?" To which Dixie replied, "Why, thank you. You are so kind." The show was an absolute scream! If you ever get a chance, do yourself a favor and go. Just don't bother telling Mother that Dixie is in drag; she won't believe you. I know, I tried.

When Mother turned seventy-nine, I decided to throw her another surprise birthday party. I called her the morning of and nonchalantly slipped into the conversation that Billy Reid was cooking that night at Primo's, an Italian restaurant in the neighborhood owned by our friend Joseph. Billy Reid helps out here and there when the kitchen is shorthanded. And we might as well get gussied up and *let* him cook for us. Ding, ding, ding! *That* was the magic word! She wasn't about to miss an opportunity to *let* someone do something for her. It was her civic duty, after all. You could even say it was her calling, her passion. She was genuinely shocked to walk in and see a sixteen-top filled with neighbors, friends, and family.

When Mother turned eighty, I decided to throw her yet another surprise birthday party. At that point, I was purely entertaining myself. I found it hysterical to see if I could catch her off guard again. A week or so prior, she started talking about wanting a hamburger from Bud's. Bud's is what we call Belle Acres. Belle Acres Golf & Country Club, to be exact. More commonly referred to as Bellyachers, it's a private, members-only place next door to where The Cupboard once stood. Requirements to join are a current member's sponsorship, an entrance fee, yearly dues, and, most importantly, a complete and utter feigning of disinterest in being involved in any shape, form, or fashion with the aforementioned establishment.

Currently, the only official member in our family is our son Porter. His coveted membership was bestowed upon him as a college graduation gift from the proprietor himself, with all of the pomp and circumstance one would expect from such an illustrious cornerstone of our fine city. Translation: Bud unceremoniously slid a key fob for entrance to Porter across the table between a half-eaten shrimp po' boy and a refilled iced tea glass while muttering congratulations. Porter thanked him by scooping it up while not looking overeager in the process.

Hiding in plain sight with an awning that has seen better days, flanked by two weather-worn gargoyle statues and overgrown weeds on a busy city street, the question I am asked most often about Belle Acres is, "Is that place still open? You can't tell from the outside." To which I respond, "Yes, and that's exactly how Bud likes it."

Okay. Where was I? Even thinking about Mother can get you off track! Oh yeah, Mother's eightieth-birthday surprise party. I called her that afternoon, fibbing that Bud was short-handed in his kitchen, and Billy Reid was going to be cooking that night. Since she'd been wanting a burger, we may as well head up there and *let* him make us one. I was speaking her love language. Mother thought nothing of it, as Bud and Billy Reid had been friends since high school, and it wasn't uncommon for them to help each other out. More than once, Bud was involved in a case of mistaken identity when I'd go looking for Billy Reid in our walk-in cooler. I'd be moving in for the kill, and Bud would pop up from bending over the produce. It would scare the hell out of both of us. One would think you could borrow a couple of tomatoes from your culinary neighbor without nearly being goosed by his wife!

I meandered into Mother's house as if we had no place to be. I even nonchalantly made other dinner recommendations. We figured we may as well take care of her burger craving and head to Bud's. We walked in and breezed past all of the official members. As Porter was still in middle school at this point, we'd yet to obtain official entrance. We made our way to a back room to dine out of the way. I slid open the door, and thirty-five people yelled, "SURPRISE!!"

She was genuinely and thoroughly shocked, scanning the room to find family and friends from near and far. There were cards and gifts and a banner for everyone to sign and write sweet messages on. Sheri Lynch—author and host of a morning drive-time radio show, a local celebrity whom I've known for years—just happened to be dining there at the same time. She was so kind and made a huge deal out of coming by and acknowledging Mother. The Queen had a grand time. On the way home, she thanked me by saying, "No more birthday parties. You've surprised me three years in a row. I don't want any more parties." To which I replied, "You're very welcome." *Asshole.*

When Mother turned eighty-five, I didn't throw her a surprise party. She complained for a month, on a loop, about "How could she possibly be eighty-five?"

and "Wasn't she just eighty?" and "Where did the time go?" and "Was I sure she was eighty-five?" and "How could five years have gone by unnoticed?" I said, "*That* is what happens when you stop celebrating. Celebrations are expressions of gratitude, and more begets more." Without hesitation, she said, "I think you outta start my birthday parties again."

You wish, lady.

Apple, Tree, Orchard

On Billy Reid's fiftieth birthday, Mother called us
to come to her house. I thought to myself, *Wow!
She remembered! I can't believe she's going to
acknowledge his big day.* Don't worry; the Earth
hadn't tipped on its axis, and the universe was still in
order. That was *not* why we were summoned. It was
business as usual.

"Hey, Billy. Have you put on weight? It sure looks
like you have," she started right in. "Oh, happy
birthday. I wrote your check. Don't forget to get it."
Birthday checks were the most intimate Mother
ever got in her relationships. Everyone received the
customary $100 with *Happy Birthday* written in the
memo line. Every great once-in-a-while, if she was
feeling especially celebratory, you'd get a bonus to
commemorate a milestone birthday, such as $116, or
$121, or in this case, $150.

She then turned her attention to me and paid him
no more nevermind. "Tonya, I want to talk to you
about buying Scott and Christopher a duplex in the
neighborhood." I was standing in her kitchen, fully
engaged in our conversation and simultaneously

showing up as an observer, all at once. "There's a place around the corner for sale. I'll make the down payment, but you'd have to get the mortgage and be responsible for it. I don't want anything to do with all that," she continued.

The fly-on-the-wall part of me was witnessing so many layers of what-the-hellness! Billy Reid had been dismissed. He was sitting with his arms folded across his chest, waiting to resume his day. I hadn't seen his birthday check yet. *Did she only write it for $105?!* Mother was discussing financial matters with me while completely excluding Billy Reid. She was talking about *his* kids. Even though we've raised them as *ours,* not yours and mine, you'd think she would have included him in the conversation. I mean, we're married, and if *I* had a mortgage, his ass would be on the hook for it too.

My brain works like a human calculator, and I figured out with some quickness that the mortgage we were looking at, even with Mother's generous offer of the down payment, would have the boys each needing to come up with four times what they were currently splitting in rent. I politely told her that they were twenty-one years old, I was going on thirty-six, and underwriting such a venture at that point in their lives didn't seem like a sound choice for our finances or theirs. But I made an appointment with the owner for us to see it later that afternoon, just to appease her.

After running errands, Billy Reid and I returned to Mother's early afternoon only to have her tell us to go on without her, as she was napping on the couch, already donning her nightgown and housecoat. We hopped in our old, beat-up Volvo to drive around the block. Under the guise of filling up the gas tank, Billy Reid had insisted we take the one car that barely survived the boys learning to drive to run over to see the house, versus showing up in one of our Land Cruisers.

A few minutes later, while we were waiting for the owner to arrive, I noticed an old woman meandering around the corner toward us. The closer she got, I realized *it was Mother!* I'd recognize that ratty-ass rag of a housecoat anywhere. What initially threw me off was how she was wearing a head full of Velcro rollers! Yep! That was Mother. Most women her age would have thrown on some street clothes and added a swipe of lipstick before going to potentially make a real estate transaction. Not her. Nope. She helped herself into the driver's seat as Billy Reid was already surveying the property. I took one look at her and offered to take her rollers out of her hair before the guy got there.

She leaned over the armrest that separated us, got within two inches of my face, looked me dead in my eyes, and whispered in a dramatic, hushed tone, "Leave them in. We don't want this man to think we have any money."

The owner arrived, and they all recognized each other from the family restaurant, The Cupboard. After showing us the duplex, which needed more time, energy, effort, and money than we were willing to contribute, we were chit-chatting while Mother wandered off to identify the foliage in the yard. Billy Reid turned to the man and said, "I apologize for my mother looking like that. She doesn't want you to think she has any money."

I turned to Billy Reid and said, "Did you hear her say that when she was sitting in the car with me?" He replied, "No, I just know my mama." The man belly laughed and said, "That's hilarious! You know, her father was the one who taught me not to judge a book by its cover." Billy Reid replied, "Wait! What? You knew my grandfather, Theo?"

The man proceeded to tell us that his very first job was as a car salesman down the street from The Cupboard. One day, he was milling around the dealership with the sales team, and a man pulled up in a beat-up truck. The guy looked worse for wear than his vehicle, clothes tattered and dirty shoes with holes on the sides to allow his bunions to escape. The veteran salesman took one look at the rookie and said, "He's all yours. Go get 'em!"

He said that he reluctantly went outside to greet the browsing customer. "Hello, sir! Would you like to take that puppy for a spin?" To which the man replied, "No, thank you. I know what I want. I just came to get someone to tell me the best price, and I'll be back tomorrow to pick it up when I can get someone to drop me off." They spoke for a few more minutes and parted ways. Once back in the dealership, the young buck recounted the conversation, much to the razzing of the old-timers. He was met with, "Yeah, right! He didn't look like he could afford to fill the tank! Dream on, pal!" as each one put in their two cents.

The next day, the chiding continued as any car with double occupancy pulled into the lot. "Hey, your buyer's here!" rang out more than once, followed by jeers and jabs. Lo and behold, half an hour before closing time, a car pulled up, and the man from the day before jumped out. He walked into the dealership, right up to the young salesman, reached his hand into the same dingy drawers he'd had on the day before, and pulled out a fat roll of bills secured with a rubber band. The man said, "This oughta do it. I'd like my keys and title, please." It was glorious! The entire showroom stood there with mouths gaping while the salesman made the easiest, cleanest sale of his career.

Billy Reid grinned and said, "I can still see my Granddad Theo's feet hanging out the side of his shoes! That was definitely him."

Beat-up Volvo. Velcro rollers. Holey shoes. The apple doesn't fall far from the tree, nor the tree from the orchard.

Driving Miss Daisy to the Beach

As Mother started getting long in the tooth ... that expression cracks me up! Especially since she wore dentures, and half the time they weren't properly secured in her face and would come flopping out mid-sentence! As Mother started getting up there in age, we would drive her wherever she wanted to go.

Remember the 1980s movie where Morgan Freeman drove Miss Daisy, played by Jessica Tandy, around the Deep South? She, of course, was in the back seat because how else is one chauffeured? Well, Mother loved nothing more than getting all nestled in the back seat with her neck pillow and a cup of ice that she would crunch on until I thought I would lose my damn mind!

She would load up, and by load up, I mean she would spend the better part of a week piling up shit by the back door that she would need at the beach. I had the honor of loading her haul when Billy Reid dropped me off to claim her. This would consist of no less than four potted plants, two industrial-size boxes of Cheerios, an inch of milk left in the bottom of a quart jug—try as I may, she never seemed to believe me that they sell milk at the beach—various bits and pieces and nibbles of leftovers, her hard-ass Samsonite suitcase, multiple pairs of SAS orthopedic maw-maw shoes, and an assortment of random stuff she transported back and forth as an act of pretending to deal with her belongings. Once, her cargo included a crystal rose bowl in the original box that she and Bill Reid had received as a retirement gift thirty years prior. That sucker had never seen the light of day, nor did it on that trip.

Mother *loved* to announce the gas prices on our journey. She did this by gasping and pointing as if someone had been murdered and left for dead on the side of the road. I was always caught off guard and would jerk the wheel to avoid whatever impending doom I thought she was trying to bring to my attention. In a nutshell, it pretty much sucked driving her bag of bones anywhere.

Every bridge we drove over came with instructions to get in the left lane. In a previous incarnation, she must have met her demise in the likes of the Chappaquiddick. A three-and-a-half-hour trip was never completed in under five hours between potty breaks, flag stores, garden centers, and detours that included driving an alternate route past Grandma Honeycutt's old house and making me stop to knock on doors to inquire about the current residents and

"Did they know or remember her kinfolk?" as she liked to say.

NO, Mother! No one remembers or gives one single shit about any of your people that lived in that falling-down, caved-in house at the end of that country-ass road! Can we please let them get back to their homemade meth lab and get the hell on to the beach?!

Other topics Mother liked to contemplate and felt the need to share out loud in the car:

On Shopping
"I don't like Dollah Tree. I like Dollah General."

On Real Estate
"I wouldn't want to live in a house where the one next to it is falling down. *(No shit, lady! That's the unspoken rule #4, right after location, location, location!)*

On the Speed Limit
"I like for you to drive because you only go a little bit over the speed limit. I have a lead foot."

On Driving Herself to the Beach
"There's the median I drove into the last time I fell asleep driving myself to the beach."

On Nature
"There goes that cloud again."

I'm not completely sure how ADHD works in the human brain with all of its chemical nuances, but if it's ever discovered that you can actually catch it, or that it's contagious, I promise you, Mother is patient ZERO. I seriously believe Mother's thoughts originated on her lips, made their way to her ears, and finally into her cranium!

Mother always kept a stack of expired coupons in her car. She would have me stop at the Wendy's in Darlington and make me go inside, not the drive-thru, to redeem them. And by me, I mean ME, all by myself. She would remain slung up in the car awaiting my return with her senior (read: discounted) coffee and whatever snack I managed to procure from the aforementioned invalid slip of paper she'd fished out of her time capsule of a glove box.

Billy Reid always drove separately under the pretense of having two cars for convenience while we were at the beach or under protest of needing more space. When truth be told, he and Mother did not enjoy each other's company. The plan was always to get her settled, spend a night or two, head back to Charlotte for work, and go collect her the next weekend or whenever she was ready to come home. Our system worked for several years until Mother became scared to stay by herself at the beach.

On Sundays, as we got ready to pull out of the driveway, she would become like a little kid at bedtime on her first sleepaway and change her mind.

My ass would have to load up her car with all sorts of uneaten ends of loaf bread, tomato plants, newly acquired geranium plants, Samsonite, and "Don't forget my rose bowl I didn't find a place for!"

The Episode

The impetus for Mother's panic of being abandoned at the beach stemmed from "an episode." This is what old Southern women refer to as an unsavory event or flare-up of sorts. I like to think of it as losing one's shit or having a temporary freak-out. In Mother's case, it was a heart attack she was still not convinced occurred, even after stent surgery.

In May of 2001, we got a call from Grand Strand Medical Center that Mother had been transferred by ambulance to their ICU. We jumped in the car and raced to see her. My sister-in-law, Mary, and her husband, Steve, were on their way from High Point, North Carolina. I could tell that our ETA, being fifteen minutes before theirs, was driving Mary insane.

Billy Reid was flying down the road like a bat out of hell and got pulled over for speeding. Window down, registration and license in hand, Billy Reid started explaining to the officer before he was fully in view that we were rushing to the hospital where his mother was taken for a heart attack, that he didn't even know why he was going so fast because they didn't get along, and that she's awful and makes him crazy. The highway patrolman heard all he cared to, patted the car, and with a verbal warning told us to take it easy. We still managed to maintain our lead.

When we arrived at the theater-in-the-round—that is what an ICU looks like to me, a semicircle of curtained rooms with the nurse's station command center positioned in the middle to keep a watchful eye on everyone—I found Mother holding court. She excitedly introduced me to her nurse, Bill. Perhaps you're wondering how I remember his name. Well, my husband, father, father-in-law, grandfather, and cousin are all some form of William, so it stuck in my noggin.

She was lit up like a firecracker, dizzy with all the attention she had been receiving. She reported that she'd become lightheaded after her morning walk and began sweating profusely while talking to a neighbor. So much so that the neighbor called 911. Mother did NOT think it was necessary because she had NOT had a heart attack!

To which Nurse Bill replied, "Yes, you did, Mrs. Reid, and the cardiologist will be in shortly to talk to you and your family. Can I get you anything else?"

Mother didn't skip a beat, as she was not one to miss an opportunity to be catered to, and said, "Bill, be a dea-yah and go get me some more of that crushed ice." Because that is what you do if you are Martha Reid holding court in a busy ICU. You use valuable resources to make sure that your every extraneous whim and desire be met as if you were Platinum Elite status at the gawd damn Ritz Carlton!

I was standing at the nurse's station inquiring about visiting hours when Mary Delight came waltzing in like the heir apparent to the Queendom. She came bursting around the corner at full stride. Right hand clutching her pocketbook—yes, purses are pocketbooks and pants are britches around here—on her shoulder and her left arm swinging, somehow propelling her forward and keeping her balanced all at the same time.

She announced her arrival by bellowing, "Does anyone know who Momma's power of attorney is?"

I nearly busted a gut laughing and replied, "Why don't you go ask her for yourself? She's right over there enjoying some crushed ice that Nurse Bill just brought her."

Visiting hours were every other hour starting on the odd hour: one o'clock, three o'clock, and five o'clock. You get the idea. It being twelve thirty, we said our goodbyes and promised to return at five with some contraband meal because, after all, Mother was convinced her cardiac event was fake news. As always, Mary Delight had her own agenda. Her second question to me, after Mother's legal affairs, was if I had thought to stop by the shop, as she liked to refer to my salon, and grab some hair color to cover her gray as we passed the time between hospital visits.

Why no, Mary, even to a seasoned hairdresser like myself, my first instinct in a medical emergency is not to stock the trunk with tubes of color and bottles of peroxide in case my assistance is needed in a triage situation!

Mary never reminded me more of her mother than in that instant. What is the old adage? The self-absorbed apple doesn't fall very far from the narcissistic tree?

So off to the drugstore we went. Much to Mary's disbelief, I was not familiar with store-bought, boxed color. (I can attest with authority that there *is* some science behind being a colorist, which extends beyond elaborate marketing campaigns making the consumer think that every person on the planet who purchases Clairol Level 6 Ash will look exactly like the happy lady on the box). Next, we proceeded to Mother's backyard. Billy Reid was taking a nap, which is code for "checked out." Mary and I invited Steve to our substitute salon on the deck.

I don't know if people really understand the power of a salon, the sanctity of it. Whether it is on 5th Avenue or some two-by-fours at the Redneck Riviera, the energy is matched only by a confessional booth in church or the couch in a therapist's office. It is a place where secrets are revealed, jokes are told, stories are shared, shit is gotten off chests, and advice is given and received. A place where folks feel seen, heard, and affirmed.

To that end, my brother-in-law used the space to share his disdain for our mother-in-law. He started with, "I hope there is a special seat in hell with Martha Reid's name on it, because I hate that woman."

I thought to myself, *Wow, Steve! Who tinkled in your gin and tonic?*

In all fairness, I was only a couple of years into the family, and Steve had nearly four decades of dealing with her. I'd love to share the nitty-gritty of how he came to feel the way he did. I can recount it in great detail, which I did in an earlier draft that I read to Billy Reid.

His reaction was, "Everything you said was 100 percent true, and you can't print it. It's okay to air our dirty laundry; just don't pile shit on it. Don't erase it. Just sit with it for now. But you cannot use it."

At first, I justified that the in-laws I'm writing about are mostly dead. Let me rephrase that: The ones that are dead are all the way dead! It's the ones that aren't that are giving me cause for pause. I explained to Billy Reid how the writer Anne Lamott always says that if you're worried about how people are going to react to the way you write about them, then they should have behaved better.

After sleeping on it, I had some revelations on the matter. Although what I'd recounted was true, it was unkind. It didn't reveal the best in anyone involved. Including me in my retelling of it. Mean is easy. As my dear friend Clark says, "Punching low doesn't require much finesse." Anne Lamott was right. They should have behaved better. Then again, maybe I should too. Once more, what happens in the salon stays in the salon, no matter how makeshift.

Plus, there's always karma to contend with, which I am constantly reminded of. The very next day, not even twenty-four hours after I came to terms with the cutting-room floor keeping the dirtiest of details, Billy Reid and I went to lunch at Lupie's, one of our favorite local lunch haunts. It's the kind of place where you don't look for the sanitation grade because you don't really want to know. Instead, you just embrace the character and vibe of it all. Everyone there looks like they once drove a VW van and served in Vietnam. We've frequented it countless times in over thirty years.

While walking in, I notice a well-dressed older couple coming in behind us. They caught my attention because they weren't the usual diners I expected to see there. Our eyes locked. Lo and behold! It was my brother-in-law Steve's sister and her husband! We had always lived in the same city, and never, not once, had I ever run into them! In fact, I'd only been in their presence a half dozen times, and the majority of those were at out-of-town events for my in-laws!

Anne Lamott can think what she wants regarding writing about people and their behavior! I'm just here to tell you that if they're deceased, they might have

time on their hands to send a proxy to remind you
to simmer down on the details of your recollections,
Miss Missy!

ᴳoing to the ᴰoctor for ᔆport

Ⓞnce Mother was back home and her stent surgery was behind her, it was time for her follow-up. This marked the beginning of her *letting me* accompany her to all her medical appointments. As in, "I am going to *let* you take me to the doctah." Mother's edition of Emily Post's book on etiquette must have had a page missing. As I said before, she never said please, rarely said thank you, and I can recall her apologizing only once. It involved, in true *Mommie Dearest* form, us getting in an argument over wire hangers. Which I wanted to throw away, and she did not. "I'm gonna let you" was her go-to phrase, and she always said it like she was doing me a favor. Oh joy!

Off we went to the Sanger Clinic, *the* premier cardiovascular facility in Charlotte, for Mother's first post-op visit. Now, keep in mind, this was before we all had cell phones glued to our eyeballs, and the only entertainment in the lobby consisted of some vintage *Good Housekeeping* magazines and the occasional *Better Homes & Gardens*. Unless, of course, you had Mother. An hour and a half into my waiting room sentence, we were informed that she didn't actually *have* an appointment. They were working her into the schedule.

"Oops, I forgot to tell you that part," she turned to me sheepishly. By this point, Mother had traipsed all over the place. It was as if she were on a scavenger hunt, and between each find, it was her duty to come and inform me of her discoveries. Do you remember *The Family Circus*? It's the comic strip that often shows the little boy being told to go get the mail out of the mailbox or to go borrow a cup of sugar from the next-door neighbor, and there's a dotted line overview of his route, which meanders all over town and back, oftentimes returning without said task being completed. *That* pretty much sums up taking Mother anywhere.

Our visit went like this:

HER
"You see that pickcha over theyah?
That is old Doctah Sangah."
Off she went to examine the picture. On her return:
"I just went pee."

ME
"Great, Mother. Thanks for sharing."

HER
"I'm gonna go get a cup of coffhey."

ME
"Okay. Have fun."

HER
Back again.
"I just went poop."

ME
"Well, how did that go?"

HER
"It wasn't nothin' but a little ole thing."
*Showing me a specific measurement
using her thumb and ring finger as a visual.*
"I'm gonna go look at other pickchas
and see if I recognize anyone."

ME
"Alright, you do that. I'll be right here holding
your pocketbook and your cane, which you
obviously don't need because you've clocked
about three miles in here so far without it."

HER
"Oh yeah! Gimme that thing."
Later: "I checked. Again. It's still not our turn."

ME

"Well, I would hope not since we're still sitting out here."

HER

"You are so patient. I'm glad you're here with me and
not Billy or May-ree. I'm much calmer around you.
Billy would be mad we've waited so long, and May-ree
would be all over the place, making me nervous. You
know?" (Yes, she actually confessed this out loud!) "I
don't particulahly enjoy being around my children."

ME

"I wouldn't worry about it too much. I can't speak for Mary,
but I can guarantee the feeling is mutual for Billy Reid."

HER

"Hmmm. I suppose you're right."

One of my clients worked the desk at the clinic.
She was there that day and was thrilled that she got
to meet Mother in the flesh and see firsthand all of
the antics she'd heard about over the years. Months
later, at one of her hair appointments, she had one of
her own Mother stories to share.

There happens to be a Chick-fil-A in the same
office building as the Sanger Clinic. It's in the middle
of a huge hospital campus, and there is an extremely
long line at all times with a captive audience of
doctors, nurses, patients, and the lucky ones who *get*

to come along with their loved ones. One day, as my client was waiting her turn with the lunch hour clock ticking away, she noticed this slight, white-haired, little old woman walk in, cut to the front of the line, wave a dollar bill in the cashier's face—oblivious to the sea of humanity rotting in line in hopes of obtaining a #1 combo sandwich, fries, and a drink with time to choke it down before returning from whence they came—and demand a "senyah size" (because it's the same as a small one but at a reduced price) ice cream in a cup.

My client said it was the most amazing thing she'd ever witnessed. We laughed our asses off! *That* was Mother. Everywhere she went, she commanded her environment like a horse whisperer or a lion tamer by playing innocent and acting pitiful. Unless she didn't. And then she'd decide she wasn't going there or doing business with *those* people ever again!

Those People

One day, Mother decided that she was going to *let* me take her to get her ears checked and see about getting hearing aids. I, of course, did not mind taking her. I told her, though, if she was just looking for an outing, I could think of a hundred other things we could do. Nope! She assured me she was ready to give hearing aids a try. I thought, *Good grief, Woman! Here we go! I'm about to waste another day off carting your ass to a doctor's office, knowing full and damn well that you have no intention of doing anything they suggest! You're just going because the rest of us taste like chicken, and you're ready for a new flavor of the month!*

I do not remember the name of the doctor we saw, but I should, because he is my hero. It was the singular most delightful medical experience that I ever had with Mother. He had her number from the get-go. This was not his first daughter-in-law-time-wasting, attention-seeking-old-lady rodeo! He gave her a hearing test and determined that, due to her limited auditory capacity, she was an excellent candidate for hearing aids.

Now the fun part (for Mother). He sat and talked to her extensively. He wanted to know all about her hearing history. Whether or not it included previously owning hearing aids. Telling her to tell him everything. Which she did. I thought she was going to tell him every word she'd ever heard uttered.

Mother. Was. In. Heaven.

I. Was. In. Hell.

She went on and on and on. She found him mesmerizing. She was doing that flirty thing she does when she has someone's full attention. Her Leo the Lioness astrological sign was loving every minute of it.

I'm pretty sure I zoned out. I was contemplating, *Has anyone ever actually gotten their eyeballs stuck in the back of their heads from rolling them? Did it involve surgery? Would it be covered on my insurance, or would it be considered elective? And if it did occur, did it happen when they took their mother-in-law to a doctor's appointment while listening to her wade through a pile of bullshit?*

At that point, my possible new-future-father-in-law-hearing-aid-doctor-dude, from the way Mother was batting her eyelashes, had her eating out of his hand. And BAM! That man took out a piece of paper and told Mother that he was going to write up a contract, and she was going to sign it before he even considered fitting her for hearing aids. *Uh oh!* I was thinking, *Do I need to call Billy Reid? Do we need*

*to contact a lawyer? Have my eyes glazed over to the
point that Mother is signing a promissory note to
the family farm? Is he expecting her to come with a
dowry? What'd I miss?*

He proceeded to write down things like:

"Dr. So-and-So"—*damn, what was his name?*—"is in charge.

I, Martha Reid, am not in charge.

I will not waste said doctor's time.

I will wear my hearing aids."

And ten other things with an X and a line for her to
sign her name.

He pretty much came up with a laundry list, right
there on the spot, of all the do's and don'ts for a
successful and rewarding patient/doctor experience,
where the doctor is undeniably in charge, and the
patient, having not been to medical school, would not
get to dictate the situation. I know I'm showing my
age, but you know the sound a record player makes
when a song is playing and someone abruptly moves
the arm, and the needle scratches across the album
as if signaling, "We're done here"?

That is precisely how the office visit ended. Mother
refused to allow the doctor to be in control. The
doctor told Mother he did not want her business
because it would be mutually unsatisfying, and that
he'd seen her type, and that he chose not to work
with *those* people. Did I hear that right? Did Mother

just get the *those* people card played on her?! Karma is a dish best served cold *and* in the presence of your daughter-in-law.

I looked that audiologist dead in the eyes and said out loud, because Mother couldn't frigging hear me anyway, "I think you are my new best friend." He grinned at me in a knowing way, the way only a kindred spirit can. I happily collected my stunned and shunned mother-in-law, and in one fell swoop, whisked her out the door before she had a chance to fully process that someone had beaten her at her own game.

A couple of years later, she thought it would be great fun for me to waste a few of my Mondays off. Mondays are a hairdresser's Sundays, so lucky me, I was available to do her bidding. She decided she wanted to go see that doctor again about hearing aids. For real, this time. No way! No how, Lady! I reminded her that he didn't want to mess with her if she was determined to be in charge.

Undeterred, we set off to Charlotte Eye, Ear, Nose & Throat in search of our next unwitting audiologist. (Don't you just love it when you can pronounce the name of a company, and their sign lets you know precisely what they're in the business of?) We were scheduled with a wonderful young hearing specialist who was new to the practice. So patient. So kind. So oblivious to Mother's tactics. First things first, the hearing test revealed that Mother had 56 percent hearing loss in one ear and 48 percent in the other. She was dumbfounded. Total shock and disbelief. You'd have thought she was given five minutes to live.

Jiminy Friggin Christmas, woman! What did you think she was going to tell you? "Ma'am, you have supersonic hearing and can detect a cockroach toot from a tree in your backyard while you're listening to your TV in the den. By the way, you've blown out the speakers because you have the volume set on a thousand AND closed captioning is scrolling across the screen!"

Misery was Delighted with a capital D! "Oh, yes," she said, "we can come back for a fitting next Monday and a follow-up the week after that! And oh, you, Miss Sweet Ear Doctor Lady, are determined to work with us to make sure this time is a successful, satisfying experience?" Ha! We'd see about THAT! Honey, Martha Reid was a professional medical appointment maker and goer, the likes of whom you have never seen! She'd have you contemplating early retirement faster than you can say, "Are my student loans paid off yet?"

Thus, Queen Mother began her reign. We went to a fitting appointment. We returned for the actual acquistion of said hearing aids. We returned for the these-things-won't-stay-in-my-ears appointment. We returned for the how-do-you-change-the-batteries-in-these-things-again appointment. On one particular visit—yes, I said *visit*. Isn't that what we're doing?

Going to visit with our friends at the clinic because they all knew us by sight, and we knew them all by name, and weren't they just the sweetest, and didn't they just fawn all over Mother?

Anyway, as I was saying, on one particular visit, we were waiting and waiting and waiting ... *Uh oh*, I thought, *they're on to you, Mother; this gig is about up.* And in comes this elderly gentleman pushing his wife in a wheelchair. The woman was slumped over, practically incoherent. She'd clearly had a stroke, or four. She reminded me of Popeye's girlfriend, Olive Oyl, raven-haired, tall, slim, about to slide out of her seat into a puddle on the floor at any moment. A normal person would have looked at someone like that with compassion or, at the very least, averted their eyes. Not Mother.

She said loudly enough for the entire waiting room to hear her (because she still refused to wear her hearing aids), "DO I LOOK AS BAD AS THAT WOMAN DOES? I SWEAR I JUST DON'T GET AROUND LIKE I USED TO. MY FEET HURT. MY BACK HURTS."

Really? You're comparing yourself to someone who looks like she died and they forgot to bury her? I just chuckled and said, "I think you're going to be okay."

Mother never did get the hang of wearing hearing aids. Even when she tried, I inevitably found them resting on her shoulders, and she was oblivious that they had fallen out. One day I was bitching to my brother-in-law Steve about how much of my precious time on this earthly plane I had been wasting on Mother and her hearing aids. He laughed and informed me that she had, in fact, purchased a pair of hearing aids ten years prior and that I should ask her about her experience.

I was furious! The next time I saw her, I said, "So Steve tells me that you bought hearing aids ten years ago. Hmm. Tell me about *that*."

Mother replied, "Oh, I hated those things! I bought a pair, put them in my ears, and drove home. I could not believe how loud my turn signal sounded! It almost drove me crazy! Everything was so loud! I got home and put them in a drawer. I just decided I didn't want to hear all that."

Please, God in heaven, I thought, *kill me now. I do not know what I am going to do with this woman. And Steve, I'm startin' to feel ya, man.*

Booty Duty

One year, at the insistence of her accountant, Mother started gifting each of us with a nice check, ya know, "for tax purposes." And one by one, we were informed by our respective banks that the checks were put on hold. I decided to talk to our personal banker at Wachovia (now Wells Fargo) to figure out what was going on. From what Julie could tell, Mother had written a large check from her Bank of America account, deposited it into a somewhat dormant account she held there at Wachovia, and immediately wrote out several checks, bringing the balance back to its former, paltry amount. With no current signature card on file, it set off red flags left and right, and all transfers came to a standstill. And rightly so.

While I was super-sleuthing as best as I could at the bank, and with Julie divulging as much information as she legally could, Mother called me all in a panic. I thought she must have been upset about the bank mix-up, so I started right in with what I had discovered. BUT (one T, not two)—if this were made for TV, I'd cue the foreshadowing music—financial matters were the least of her concerns at the moment.

She started in with, "You know that hemorrhoid prescription you picked up for me the other day? Well, you or Becky, you know, because Becky used to be a nurse, need to come over here and do it for me. I can barely wipe myself. There's no way I can apply this medicine."

"Um, excuse me, Mother. We need to do *what*? We need to put hemorrhoid medicine on your butt?"—two Ts, not one—"Can I call you in a few minutes after I'm finished at the bank?" I incredulously inquired.

Once home, I called her back. At that point, another ailment had grabbed her attention. She informed me that her foot had kept her up all night, throbbing. She was able to obtain a last-minute cancellation appointment at the podiatrist if she could be there within the hour, and she needed me to take her. I told her that I was due at the salon for several meetings and that I would send Billy Reid to take her.

Billy Reid's ears perked up hearing the mention of his name. I told Mother to hold on and covered the mouthpiece of the phone with my hand. He yelled, "I'm not taking her! I hate this city, and I hate my momma! I've got a buddy pass from Angela Price, and I'm getting the hell out of here for the day. I thought I'd go to Disney and ride rides! You have meetings all day, and I'll be back in time to go to dinner."

Let me explain. Angela Price is a long-time family friend who is a self-proclaimed Super Stewardess Extraordinaire, and she's not mistaken. She's one of those people who was born in the wrong era. She should have been fanned by dedicated ladies-in-waiting or adoring suitors, or at the very least flown the friendly skies in the midst of the space age when being a flight attendant was the epitome of glamor. Even though that was not the hand she was dealt, somehow she manages, in this day and time, to maintain a level of charm and decorum with her red lipstick intact and not a hair out of place while she serves the front of the plane like it's still 1965, versus slinging drinks and passing out pretzels on the bus with wings that her industry has become. She also happens to be Billy Reid's supplier of buddy passes when he's had enough and needs to get the heck outta town for a minute! A supply of readily available plane rides that made becoming a Disney season passholder a no-brainer! At least that's our rationale. Some husbands drink, golf, gamble, or all three! Not Billy Reid. Disney it is. If he's happy, I'm happy.

But not that day! I gave him one last mean mug (you know, the glare that suggests heads are gonna roll), released my hand from the phone, and said, "Get dressed, Mother. Billy Reid will be there in fifteen minutes to get you to your doctor appointment on time."

On my way to work, I checked in with Mother again. I told her that she needed to quit wandering around the house worrying about her booty medicine and get dressed. To which she replied, "How did you know I was doing that?" To which I responded, "Well, I've met you." I said that Billy Reid was going to be there any minute, and she didn't want to put the podiatrist *behind*—I have to entertain myself here, people, or I might actually start slitting throats —because he'd so kindly worked her in, and to quit getting herself worked up. I would stop by after work, and we'd figure out her prescription together. She told me that it was a seven-day supply. I told her that since it was Friday, I'd come by that day and every day for a week to help her, and by Thursday, it would be over with. Easy peasy.

This entire hemorrhoid fiasco started a few weeks earlier when I was toting her on some other errand, and she announced that she had The Cansah. I asked her if an actual physician had diagnosed that she, in fact, had cancer. She shook her head no, said that she was bleeding from her rectum, and that she was too afraid to go to the doctor because she just knew she had cancer. Here's the funny thing about going to the doctor when you habitually go to help kill a few hours in the day: When you suspect something might actually be wrong, it takes all of the fun out of it.

Long story longer, I *end up*—it's the gift that keeps on giving—taking her to the proctologist. Only we didn't see the proctologist. We saw his PA, which is fine, one would think, except looking *back*—gotcha again—he didn't physically examine Mother. We just sat and talked. He had her chart and the results from her most recent colonoscopy, which were less than a year old. He told us that everything looked clear there, and based on the symptoms she reported, we were dealing with an ordinary hemorrhoid. He would prescribe some medicine, and we were good to go.

On the way back to the car, I said, "Mother, isn't that great? See, you don't have cancer after all. You have so much to be grateful for."

She sighed, "I suppose I *should* be grateful, but I *do* have a hemorrhoid."

Where was I? Oh yeah. Easy peasy. Right? Wrong!! After work, I stopped by Mother's house as promised. You know that saying, "No good deed goes unpunished"? They were talking about doing *anything* for my mother-in-law! Mother informed me that upon further study of the instructions, it said to apply the medicine to her backside TWICE a day! So that meant I had unknowingly committed myself to going over morning and night to spray hemorrhoid-shrinking potion up her ass fourteen times! Count 'em! 1-4! As in 14!

We started right then and there. She plopped on her bed. I placed her stick figure face-down in the shape of a lowercase letter *h*, with her arms over her head out of the way and her right knee hiked up so I could see what was going on in those cheeks of hers. Donned with gloves, I foamed her up and got the hell outta there. Yelled over my shoulder that I'd see her in the morning, escaping to my car before the door had a chance to hit me in the ass!

I went back early the next day, before my busy Saturday at the salon. I returned worn out that evening. Billy Reid waited for me in the car in her driveway because we were going to dinner afterward, and he refused to come inside. Mother acknowledged that he was out there and thought nothing of him staying put. There was no love lost for either party. Mother was too busy entertaining her neighbors, who looked like they had become part of the furniture. Lee and Al, from two doors down, were, in my approximation, one hundred twenty-five and one hundred twenty-seven years old, respectively. Mother was downright giddy from all of the attention. They had come over to check on her, and she had been entertaining them with stories of going to the podiatrist and proctologist and my upcoming "visits" to treat her bum. You'd have thought she was deemed Prom Queen of the Century by AARP by the look on all of their faces. Mother told them in a sing-songy voice not to go anywhere while we went down the hall to do her medicine and that she'd be right back. Lee grabbed me by my arm and looked at me like I was the Chosen One, telling me what a good girl I was. *You have no idea, lady!*

I was there bright and early the next day. Mother wasn't nearly as chipper. It's like she had a hangover from riding high the night before. She told me that her foot was still bothering her, the podiatrist totally dismissed her on Friday, and Lee and Al were going to take her to urgent care because they knew the sweet staff that worked there on Sunday mornings. *Oh, I bet they do, Mother, I bet they do!* I told her to have fun, and I'd see her later, foaming her fanny as fast as I could before she had a chance to invite me to tag along.

I returned that evening, and she announced that she had The Shingle. Singular with a capital "The" added for emphasis. Makes it sound all the more tragic. And perhaps it won't hurt as badly or last as long if there's only one of them. As she lay limp atop the covers in her lowercase *h*, she started whimpering and feeling sorry for herself. She cried out, "Tonya, you have no idea how terrible all of this is for me!" To which I blurted out, "It's no picnic on my end either!" We both dissolved into a puddle of laughter. What else can you do in such an absurd situation?!

We settled into our routine. Monday morning. Monday evening. Once there on Tuesday morning, I informed her I'd be later than usual that evening, as I had a prior engagement after work. She thought it would be okay to skip a treatment. Wednesday morning. Wednesday evening. Thursday morning. That day at work, I was the one who was giddy. By then, my clients had been thoroughly entertained by my latest Mother shenanigans, and I even had a celebratory Booty Duty Dance to express my elation at ending my tenure as nursemaid. I only had one more dose to administer, and I'd be done, forever, with Mother's nether region. Or so I thought.

I got there Thursday night, and Mother started talking to her dog, saying things like, "We sure are going to miss Tonya's little visits, aren't we, Millie? It's been so nice having her over to get us going in the morning and to tuck us in, in the evenings."

I said, "Is that what you call me squirting lotion in your bunghole all week? Little visits?! Christ on a cracker, lady! If you want visitors, there are easier ways to make that happen!"

She paid me no attention, and to my utter horror, I began to realize that she had already decided *she* would be the one to say when I was done, and as far as she was concerned, we were not done here. Already plotted out, she explained, "Well, the directions said twice a day. You only did it once on the first day because you didn't come over until *after* your meetings. *And* you didn't come over Tuesday night because you had plans. I checked, and there's plenty left in the bottle, so you need to come back twice tomorrow."

I left deflated. I had no more Booty Duty Dance pep left in my step. I didn't think I could be more irritated with my day until I walked into my home. Greeting me at the door, Billy Reid announced that he'd checked the flights for the next day, and as luck would have it, there was room for him to catch a ride to Orlando and back, since *he* had to take Mother to the foot doctor the week before.

I dropped him off at the airport the next morning. Yes, I put it in park before he got out. No, I didn't accidentally, on purpose, drive in a circle, repeatedly using him as a speed bump. Remember that lady who did that to her husband in a hotel parking lot years ago? I think it was in Texas. Anyway, you can Google it. *Hmmmm, I wonder how she and her mother-in-law got along?*

Okay, okay. Let me wrap this up for you, if you're still with me. I dropped Billy Reid at the airport and booked it to Mother's. I found her sitting at the kitchen table, leisurely reading her paper and eating her Cheerios. Breakfast for her was a ritual. She had a house full of china, Corelle, various bowls and dishes left over from years in the restaurant business, and she ate her cereal out of a two-cup measuring cup with a handle and a big-ass serving spoon. There was an elaborate process to it. Her two-cupper with three-quarters of a cup of skim milk, four ice cubes (small ones, not big ones—never fill the ice tray all the way, only halfway), her huge spoon, and a box of Cheerios. She would dispense a few pieces of cereal, slosh them around in her iced milk concoction, fish them out even fewer at a time, and slurp them off the edge of her spoon loud enough to wake the dead. Then she'd continue to add cereal until the cup was bone dry. All in all, it took her about an hour and a half to finish breakfast.

From the amount of liquid still in her measuring cup, I figured I may as well pull up a seat because I wasn't going anywhere anytime soon. At that point, I noticed she had her checkbook out. I said, "Oh yeah, we haven't talked about the checks you wrote everyone last month that didn't clear the bank. Julie from Wachovia said I could run you by to fill out a current signature card, so you could just rewrite the checks, and everything should be good to go. Would you like for me to help you do that now?" This wasn't an out-of-the-ordinary conversation for us to have, as she had been relying on me for a few years to help her balance her bank statements and pay her bills. She called it "working on her table," as that was where she kept everything piled up.

"No!" she said. "I'm not worried about that right now. I have my checkbook out because I want to pay you for coming over here this week and helping me with my medicine. Hmmm. What do you think is a good price? I was thinking ten dollars a visit. So that would be a hundred and forty total."

I sat there speechless, which is rare for me. My mind was going in a million different directions! *A hundred and forty dollars? Are you kidding me? First of all, I didn't do it to get paid! Secondly, if I were to get paid what it was worth, you'd better be adding a comma and some damn zeroes, Sister Friend! Lastly, are you really not gonna deal with your banking issue now? It'll be dragged out, making me come by to visit*

a couple more times to get that all squared away.
All I could manage to squeak out was, "I don't think you can afford me. How about you just finish your breakfast so we can get a move on?"

The second thing I noticed that morning, while administering dose thirteen of fourteen, was that there was no decrease in the size of her hemorrhoid. If anything, it looked bigger to me. And I told her as much. I'm not a doctor or a pharmacist or even a nurse, so I just chalked it up to the medicine taking a minute to do its thing. All I knew was that I had one more check-in that evening before I made parole, I was going to pick Billy Reid up from the airport, and my buttocks bucks were paying for dinner! Things were looking up!

Putting the Pro in Rectal Prolapse

Imagine my excitement when Mother called me the following week to let me know that the proctologist had referred her to a colorectal specialist. She'd thought about what I'd told her regarding the size of her hemorrhoid. After a few phone calls to the pharmacist and the doctor's office, Mother was told that the medicine should have helped immediately, especially with our diligent application schedule. In fact, her hemorrhoid should have been completely gone! There was some cause for concern, and we were to go see the specialist. Pronto.

So come Monday ... it'll be alright ... sorry! That's a Jimmy Buffett song. Does anyone else go through life hearing song lyrics as a coping mechanism for dealing with life's inconveniences? I was going to say life's shitshows, but I may have used up my pun punch card telling y'all about my booty duty!

Anyway, Monday rolled around, and I showed up at Mother's house to take her to see the specialist. We got to his office, and there sat her best friend,

Becky, waiting for us. I greeted her, and Mother said, "Oh yeah, I forgot to tell you that I had Becky come meet us for my appointment. You know, because she used to be a nurse and all." From the looks of it, I was pretty certain Mother hadn't told Becky that I was coming too. It kind of felt like Queen Bee-hind had her entourage at the butt doctor.

I was having a hard enough time sitting there, having not fully recovered from dealing with Mother's rear end only days ago. Plus, I found out the doctor's name sounded awfully close to Dr. Gerbil. I won't divulge his name, as he is a lovely human being and is still running a highly successful practice in the area, providing much-needed care. And it's not his fault that my sense of humor is akin to a middle school boy's and that I still snicker at potty jokes. He couldn't help that my mind was racing with curiosity about whether it is actually possible to accidentally sit on a gerbil or a pool cue or any other odd urban myth I'd heard about. It was all beyond me with my own personal, strict, no in-the-out-door policy! No way! No how! No, thank you!

The nurse retrieved us from the waiting area, and we all squeezed into a tiny examining room. She had Mother strip from the waist down, climb on the narrowest table I've ever seen at a doctor's office, and lie on her side under a sheet. She assured us the doctor would be right in. The table seemed so slim, and to ensure that Mother didn't roll right off, Becky stood on her front-facing side, and I, knowing my role and accepting my lot in life, had Mother's back, as always.

Dr. Rectal Correctal came in and made Mother feel at ease. Mother introduced her wingwomen. We told him about her self-imposed cancer scare, our visit to the proctologist's PA, our week-long medicine regimen, and the follow-up concerns that brought us in to see him. With that, he asked to take a peek to get to the *bottom*—I know. I can't help it. It's a knee-jerk reaction—of what was going on. He told her that he was going to test the muscle strength of her rectum and that she might feel some pressure.

He reported back that her muscles were nice and tight, to which I inquired, did he happen to find her wallet in there? We both snickered, and Mother said, "What did you say?" Because, of course, she wasn't wearing her hearing aids. I responded louder with, "He said your rectum is nice and tight, and that's a good thing!"

He finished his assessment, rolled back his chair, and snapped off his gloves. He reported, "You never had a hemorrhoid, Mrs. Reid. You have rectal prolapse."

I said, "Wait a minute. You mean to tell me that I applied hemorrhoid-shrinking medicine to her fourteen times for an entire week for absolutely no reason because it wasn't a hemorrhoid in the first place? And come to think of it, the PA never took a look at it for himself to confirm that it was or was not a hemorrhoid. And what is actually happening is that her ass is falling out of her ass?!?!"

With a big grin on his face, he confirmed, "Yes! That is exactly what happened. I mean, that's not what we call it, but essentially that's what it is. The course of treatment is a tiny little band that I will place around the fissure. I will do that repeatedly until the blood supply is cut off, the protrusion shrinks, and it falls off. You'll need to bring her in every three weeks for the foreseeable future. It may take up to several visits."

I was too busy throwing up in my mouth a little bit to protest. And Mother was ecstatic to have something to look forward to. She skedaddled off the table in record time to go fill her calendar with upcoming appointments, while I offered up a silent prayer to the powers that be. *Please, please, please, may I ascend to another realm before my butt outstays its usefulness on this plane of existence!*

Get the Fuck On, Mimi

Sometimes, I have to actually go to my *own* doctor's appointments. I also have a terrible habit of leaving my house at *exactly* the right amount of time to make it to appointments, minus five or six minutes. You can set your watch to my tardiness. Just five or six minutes, that's all.

I've read so many articles about time management, punctuality, and habitual lateness. There are all of these theories about the mindset of a repeat overdue offender. Total disregard for other people's time. Lack of respect. Overinflated sense of self-importance. None of these even remotely enter my psyche as I'm twirling through my kitchen, purse slung over my shoulder, juggling keys, coffee, and whatever I need for my meetings. I'm like a whirling dervish, switching the laundry over, starting the dishwasher, and trying to put as many things as possible back in their rightful places on my way out the door.

As per usual, on one particular morning in the car, I popped an address into my navigation system and opted for the fastest of three possible routes to take me to my consultation. My glorious, long-awaited consultation with a bioidentical hormone replacement doctor. A menopause wizard who was guaranteed to abolish my hot flashes, restore my sleep, and help me remember where I had misplaced my waistline. I had eleven minutes to get to my appointment, thirteen minutes away. Would you look at that?! If everything went my way, if the stars were aligned, if everyone got the HELL out of my way, I was going to be right on time!

That particular route (although every satellite in the cosmos assured me otherwise) was causing me some doubt about my selection. A mere four office building driveways from my destination was a historically long left-turn lane, with a quick-changing light at a notoriously busy intersection, where the cross-traffic lights stayed green for what felt like an eternity. I'd never been to a rodeo, but I could feel my adrenaline pumping like a cowboy on a bucking bronco waiting to be let out of the pen to rope a bull. Only I was a sleep-deprived fifty-two-year-old lady with the air conditioning on blast in my 275 horsepower Land Cruiser, trying not to sweat through my undergarments while calculating how many cars were in front of me and whether or not they'd have the ballsacks to make the light.

The cage opened! I mean, the light changed, and I was READY! My eyes were darting between the traffic light and the brake lights of the car in front of me. Seven cars. Were we all going to make it?!

I was soooo close to my target! I heard myself yell, "FUCKING GO, LADY! GO!" At that moment, my eyes landed on her bumper, making sure I was safe to gun it through the turn. For the first time, I noticed the sticker proudly displayed on the back of her car. It ever so sweetly informed me that I had just sent darts of disgust to THE WORLD'S BEST NANA.

Who knows? Maybe she was, maybe she wasn't. Maybe she was like my mother-in-law, and she had totally destroyed her children's self-esteem, but doled out money occasionally. Plus, stores don't sell THE WORLD'S SUCKIEST NANA stickers. Either way, I was left pondering what kind of monster I had become and if there was hope left for any of us.

Run, Caregivers, Run

My generation, Gen X, is this little slice of humanity born from 1965 to 1980. We came on the scene after the baby boomers and helped usher in the millennials that followed suit. Our population is smaller than the generations before us, or since. We aren't from the "me" generation; that would be our parents. We don't belong to the "everyone gets a trophy" era; that would be our offspring and every population after us. I don't see that changing. Good luck doing away with that dynamic! We are what's known as the "sandwich" generation, since we more than likely will end up caring for our aging parents and our young children, or even our "trying their best to adult" kids, at the same time.

A friend of mine, Jane Howard, once hauntingly shared her experience with me by saying, "It's weird. It feels like we raise our children and lower our parents." She has no idea how often I've thought of that revelation she offhandedly said out loud to me during a particularly trying time in her family. She pretty much nailed it.

I personally like to call it the "panini" generation. It's just like a sandwich, but you get your face melted off between two hot-ass, rigid metal plates! It doesn't look like there's much room for what was once the contents. I may or may not have been entering menopause when that vision came to me.

As our last son was going off to college, Mother started becoming Mrs. Needy McNeederson. I was still seeing clients three evenings a week at the salon. What was once occasional, like the hemorrhoid-a-geddan episode, soon became an expectation of my presence each evening after working all day. I was starting to understand that story about boiling a frog. You place him in a pot of lukewarm water and keep turning up the temp little by little 'til he's trapped and cooked, and it's too late to escape!

"Oh, I need a little help refilling my weekly pillbox."

"I'm going to let you help me with my bank statement and the bills that are taking over my table."

"Don't go just yet. I guess I will jump in the shower like you suggested when you got here an hour ago."

"I wish you lived here with me. But not Billy. I couldn't live with him."

I often had to remind her that Billy Reid and I were a package deal. I was, after all, married to him, not her, and there's no way in hell he'd move in with her anyway. I'd walk in asking her the last time she'd showered, and if she "couldn't recall," I'd tell her that it was time. She'd hem and haw and tell me she would do it the next day, which meant, you guessed it, my ass was expected to come the next evening after work. Or oftentimes, she would say she didn't feel like it, talk about her day for an hour, and decide, as I was trying to walk out the door, that she did, in fact, want to take a quick rinse off! Pffft! There's nothing quick about corralling an octogenarian and their hygiene routine!

Soon, Mother started exhibiting odd behaviors. Or, I should say, odd even by her standards. By odd, I mean attention-seeking. Once we popped in for a visit, and while making conversation, she complained about this young woman who kept calling her. *What?! What young woman? How did she get your number? Where did you meet her? Mother, what aren't you telling us?* After quite a bit of prodding from me and more than a few "gawd damns" from Billy Reid, Mother finally spilled it.

She'd been at the Harris Teeter, our neighborhood grocery store, a week or so prior. During one of her "I need to sit down on this bench at the front of the store and look like a crazy person" breaks to rest her legs while shopping, she met a girl named Angel, whom I guess was also sitting there looking like a crazy person. She proceeded to tell us nonchalantly that Angel ended up needing a ride home, which she gave to her AND HER BOYFRIEND!

Between what I said out loud and what I thought, my brain was racing with, *What the hell's frigging bells, Mother? You did what? You drove who, what, when, and where?!?! Oh, you've seen her there often?*

Did you tell them where you live? Oh, you didn't! Well, that's something, at least! They live not too far from you. Just one neighborhood over! Did you know that you're eighty-six years old and probably shouldn't be picking up hitchhikers? Oh, and you gave her your phone number? And now she won't stop calling you? What exactly did you think was going to happen when you befriended a rando off the loony bench at the Teeter? Oh, and now you'd like us to get her to stop calling you?

Sprinkle in a few more "gawd damns" from Billy Reid and picture him pacing the floor while alternating between throwing his head back with his hands wrapped around each temple and swinging his arms down by his side with clenched fists, while intermittently holding his breath and letting out shushing sounds, looking like a human tea kettle about to explode. Mother was meekly slumped down in her chair, doing her best victim impersonation, shaking her head in disbelief that Angel was harassing her.

Billy Reid, vowing to get to the bottom of this nonsense, jumped in the car and went around the corner to see if anyone at the customer service desk could give him any more insight into who may be loitering around the front and preying on innocent little old ladies. Sherlock Holmes returned and reported that yes, the employees were familiar with Mother, and yes, they knew Angel, and that Angel was actually a grown-ass woman, which meant her boyfriend was a grown-ass man. Which meant Billy Reid was about to lose his damn mind!

I did what I often did when observing Mother and her dramatics. I remained calm. I asked as many questions as possible, because at some point, she was going to come clean about what really happened. At some point, my brain would click in, and I'd think, *Oh, now we're getting somewhere.* That was what she did. She'd get bored. She'd wander out into the world or make a pitiful plea to a passerby or a visitor. She'd end up inserting herself in a situation that would escalate beyond her interest in being involved, or someone would offer assistance that became not only unhelpful but could also take a wildly inappropriate turn.

Around that same time, my sister-in-law Mary's best friend, Lynn, stopped by for a visit after having been to an appointment with an estate attorney. Mother feigned being overwhelmed in needing to get her affairs in order. Lynn took that as poor Mrs. Reid going at it all alone. With Mother's blessing, Lynn picked up the phone and left word with the attorney's office to please contact Mother and that it was urgent. Lynn, at least, had the good sense to text Billy Reid to let him know that she was happy to help Mother plan her estate and that a lawyer was already called in to help. Billy Reid bypassed the "gawd damns," and went straight to the "what the fucks!"

Between making phone calls to various people and places—to kindly (or not so kindly if it was Billy Reid's turn to call) let it be known that Mother's will was already ironclad and that she had shuttered her shuttle service—and constantly needing to drop everything to run over and soothe her every anxious whim, we decided it was time to call in some help.

Mother had also taken to "bouts of the sundownahs," as she referred to her almost daily meltdowns around four in the afternoon, where she would go outside and hope for a passerby to notice her. It was fine for her to be outside; it just would have had more of a desired effect if she had been willing to be donned in anything other than her housecoat, ankle socks, and sensible shoes. Or maybe if she'd taken the metal chair she'd dragged from around back and placed it on the porch or the driveway, instead of stuffing it precariously in a dirt bed under the eaves where she'd peek through the bushes. I don't know, call *me* crazy, but I don't think that's what Dale Carnegie had in mind when he was coaching the masses on winning friends and influencing people!

So we began our caregiver search. Joan was overqualified. She had a leather portfolio that contained letters of recommendation, copies of her undergraduate and master's degrees in nursing, and an extensive resume. Cathy lasted two weeks. She wasn't even a blip on the radar screen. I don't even remember how we discovered Paula, Dollie, and

Ericka. I'm pretty sure that trifecta found us. And I am so grateful they did.

Paula and her mother, Dollie, are hairdressers, so I knew they were up for the task. Hairdressers are built different. They're wired for whatever. They understand how to navigate a multitude of personalities, even when said personalities are springing forth from one entity. Ericka is Paula's daughter and Dollie's granddaughter. Offspring of hairdressers are built different too. I can show you precisely where I was standing on Mother's driveway when they accepted the gig and told me how sweet Mother seemed. I didn't pull any punches and made it abundantly clear not to be snookered. My exact words were, "Beware. She's a wolf in sheep's clothing. Don't be fooled."

Their tenure started out quite well. They were great about being interchangeable. Someone came every afternoon around two and stayed until eight. Mother was thrilled with her three-pack of fresh meat! She was full of renewed life. Mother adored Dollie, and by the third "visit," as she liked to call them, she asked Dollie if she'd like to move in with her. With Mother's newfound energy, she insisted on preparing supper for whoever showed up to cover the shift that day. She was giddy with the attentiveness and was complimentary of the women when I would check in on things.

I was thrilled that Paula kept me informed of the goings-on. It was nice to have a heads-up that Dollie had been given a change of address opportunity and had respectfully declined the offer. Paula let me know that they in no way expected Mother to feed them; they always brought their own meals and beverages, and Mother always insisted on cooking for them nonetheless. Paula told me about the light cleaning and laundry she would attempt to help with and Mother's insistence that she just sit and visit with her instead. Paula also reported on any visitors that Mother may have had that day and if there was anything I needed to be made aware of, any molehills that had the potential to become mountains with Mother's penchant to defy boundaries. We had a system of logging hours, activities, and anything above and beyond that they'd handled, and I made sure they were accurately compensated.

The end of Paula and Dollie's tenure played out like so: Mother began feeling much better in the afternoons. Her anxiety had not reared its ugly head in weeks. She started calling Paula last minute— while Paula was already en route or even pulling into the driveway—to let her know there was no need to come that day. She started complaining to me about wasting money, that it was ridiculous that we'd basically hired people to be her friend. She was tired of cooking for those people. All they did was sit on their asses gabbing, and they didn't lift a finger to help do anything. The straw that broke the camel's back for Paula was when Mother's best friend, Becky, came to visit and Mother proceeded to tell Becky, while

Paula was sitting right there with them, how utterly lazy she thought Paula's daughter, Ericka, was!

Geez, frigging Louise, lady! We hired you friends because everyone else is on to you!

I've Fallen and I Can't Get Up

Once Mother ran through caregivers like a KFC bucket at a family reunion, Billy Reid and I resumed checking in on her daily, often multiple times. If she was having a spell and I had shit to do, I'd scoop her up and drag her along with me. If we found out she was wearing out the neighbors with requests, I'd spend the night and give them a reprieve.

"Yes, Mother. Your cable is out. ... No, we don't need to call John from across the street to come help. The cable is out on this entire side of the street. ... Oh, you already called him, and he came over and couldn't get it to work. ... Remember, Billy Reid came by this morning and called the cable company, and they're working on it? ... Oh, and Bill, your other neighbor across the street, came when you called, and y'all changed the batteries in your remote, and it still didn't work? ... Well, go figure."

It was getting beyond absurd. She was the girl who cried wolf! Until the wolf caught up with her. Well, not a wolf exactly, more like her driveway caught up with her. I'd been telling her for years that she would meet her demise trying to get in and out of the back door. And damn if she didn't! She had a storm door to contend with, potted plants lining the steps to the entrance, an occasional umbrella needing to be put away, the morning paper, old milk jugs to water her plants, and a myriad of wrought-iron furniture, including an oversized umbrella through the middle of an outdoor dining table, which she refused to close or open entirely. She liked to keep it contracted just enough so that it would dot you in the eye or swipe the back of your head as you were coming or going. We were all incessantly bobbing and weaving to get around it. I was constantly pulling it a few feet out to give her room, and every visitor that stopped by would hear, "Be a deayah and scooch that table a little closer to the house, would ya?" Can you say *power struggle*?!

Mother called one day and asked me to reach out to Merrywood, a cute little retirement village within walking distance of her home, and to set up a time for us to take a tour. I told her that she was never going to agree to go there, and I really didn't want to waste a moment of my time off pretending that she was. Calling her bluff only made her dig in. Finally, after a few weeks of her promising she was serious about going to live there, I made an appointment with the director, and off we went. As we were walking into the facility, Mother was admiring a unit on the bottom floor with a patio facing the parking lot. She even said that if one was unoccupied, she'd move there in a heartbeat.

Apparently, news had traveled that we were coming, and friendly faces were there to greet her. It was like old home week. Many of the residents were long-time customers of The Cupboard and were excited to see her. Mother was practically a celebrity. As we finished looking around the grounds and inspecting the model unit, the director asked Mother her timeframe. Giddy with all of the fanfare she'd received, she said that she would move in the next day if the spot she wanted was available. Well, wouldn't you know it! As luck would have it, that unit had recently become available! In fact, it'd be ready in a month. For those of you not fluent in old folks' home lingo, "recently became available" is code for someone just bit the dust.

Mother put down a hundred dollar refundable deposit and acted like she was going home to pack. The director told Mother that she would call her weekly with updates. I thought, *THIS is too good to be true.* We were barely out the door, not even to the car, and Mother turned to me and said, "I am *not* going there to live! But don't tell that nice lady because I'm going to let her call and check on me." I wanted to wring her damn neck right then and there. I imagined the satisfaction I'd have calling Merrywood to let them know that, as my luck would have it, I no longer needed that apartment for my mother-in-law.

I got a call at work about two months later. It was Billy Reid. He was on his way to the hospital. He'd been out walking and left his phone. When he returned, he heard it ringing and answered as the call dropped. It was Mother. Again. He told me he just didn't want to mess with her right then. By his calculation, he'd been to her house fifteen times in the prior six days. Just him. I'd stopped by too. He grabbed his wallet to get them lunch, and he planned on being at her house shortly. He needed a second to not deal with her. As much as he would grumble, he always did right by her and decided to call her back. She answered. She was sprawled out on her driveway. She literally—no, not literally—she *actually* knocked her teeth out of her head! Her dentures! She didn't know how, but she got tangled up coming out her back door, lost her footing, reached for that damn umbrella, and got tossed out onto the concrete. Billy Reid got to her right after the next-door neighbor, Kevin, discovered her and before the ambulance pulled in.

That evening, I found her in the ICU with a broken pelvis. She grabbed my hand and said that she wanted me to call Merrywood and see when she could move in. I told her, "No way! No how! That ship has sailed! You had your chance, and now you can't go there because they don't have rehab or long-term care." If only she had quit with her bullshit and actually gone when she was on her attention-seeking mission. A lot of places have different degrees of care, but they require that you be able to walk in unassisted. They don't care if you crash and burn that afternoon, but you have to at least present as a viable, functioning, somewhat vertical candidate from the get-go.

For the better part of a week, Billy Reid and I split time by her side. I had clients during the day, and at night, I slept in the chair in her room. We had a notebook to jot down every interaction we had with the staff. We weren't doing it to gather evidence against anyone. There was just too much going on to keep it all straight. In one day, I counted seven different people coming in to get updates, perform cognitive tests, and dole out information, many with brochures in hand. How many times was she going to be required to draw a clock and its hands, recall the date, and name the current president? Why does every shift have two nurses who actually administer care and a bazillion personnel who represent the administration? I was starting to understand the need for charging eight hundred dollars for a Tylenol. There was a lot of overhead, and very few were doing the heavy lifting.

It was becoming increasingly obvious that Mother was unable to resume living at home by herself. So off Billy Reid and I went to find the social worker in charge of putting out an all-points bulletin to the local facilities within the county limits to see who had the space for her bag of bones to go. Fortunately, Sharon Towers, one of the best retirement homes in town, had an open bed in its long-term care wing. It was the only way she would have gotten in, as they had a two-year waiting list for assisted living.

Mother always managed to skip the line and get her way. Even if it was via her face, she always landed on her feet.

Queen of the Tower

At Sharon Towers, Mother reached the pinnacle of her life's purpose: to be doted on hand and foot. Oh, how she had arrived! To the tune of eight thousand dollars per month, you too could have an entire staff. It's probably more like eleven thousand a month now, adjusted for inflation. *Hmmmm.* (Note to self: Call about a long-term care policy tomorrow!) Yes, indeed, Mother had arrived!

We got her to the point that with regular physical therapy and our coaxing, she was cruising through the halls, rubbernecking into each room as she and her walker made the rounds on the floor. She was seeing some success with her mobility until she realized that the more she could do for herself, the less the staff needed to do for her. Well, where's the fun in *that*? So *skrrrt!* That was the end of that.

Mother became beholden to her wheelchair. She wouldn't even bother to use her arms. For some reason, the old-timers there all had the footrests removed from their wheelchairs, and they used their feet to creep-crawl down the halls. They reminded me of baby turtles making their way through the sand

and out to sea. Only they were as old as Methuselah and making their way across the linoleum to the dining hall.

Mother informed me that she wanted to start wearing her diamond. *What?* I'd known this woman for nearly thirty years, and she'd only worn her diamond wedding ring on two occasions. One was years earlier on Christmas Eve when I picked her up for dinner. She saw me all gussied up, so she wanted to put on the dog too! That's Southern for getting all fancy. She had me retrieve it for her. I was instructed to go into her bedroom. On the bench, at the foot of her bed, were two hard plastic Samsonite suitcases. They had never *not* been there. She told me to open the one on the left and to find the tear in the lining on the bottom toward the back. I was ordered to fish my finger around in the hole of the satin until I pulled out a two-carat diamond ring!

Are you kidding me? If Mother had bitten the dust at any point prior to this, I'd already fantasized about loading up those mofos with as many Hummel trinkets or Madame Alexander dolls as possible, and they'd be my first deposit to the landfill! Now I realized she stored her trappings like she was some kind of kingpin preparing for a raid. Were we really going to have to go through her possessions with a fine-tooth comb someday? Kill me now!

The second time she wore her diamond was when our son Scott got married. I guess she was feeling festive and all. She wanted me to fetch it for her. I told her I knew where it was. Nope! She'd moved it! I was instructed to look in the lesser-used of her two bedroom closets. On the floor, in the back corner, I pulled out an old canvas bag, the kind companies give out for marketing purposes at trade shows. Inside was a sandwich-sized Ziploc baggie filled with folded-up tissues. In the center of the tissues, there was a smaller plastic baggie. Inside that nesting doll of a hiding place was an additional single tissue, which I unfolded to reveal her ring. *Are you for real right now, lady? Am I really going to have to go through every fiber in here when you eat it?!*

Mother loved her belongings. I'd always joke and say that you would know when Martha Reid left the planet because she was the one person in the history of ever that would figure out a way to take all of her stuff with her, and there would be a hole to the center of the Earth where all of her shit once stood. *Oh, please, please, please, let that be true!*

So when Mother wanted to start being bedazzled and bejeweled, I told her, "No way, no how." She said, "Well, I want the people here to know I have money." Billy Reid told her, "If your ass is in here, it means you have money."

All this was coming from a woman who had spent her entire existence looking practically homeless. For years, one of her prized wardrobe staples was an old blue jacket Bill Reid got from Sears that he wore until it was threadbare. When she took ownership of it, the back had split, and she mended it by slapping on a six-inch piece of silver duct tape. She wore it everywhere until one evening, her neighbors, Anne and Kevin, encouraged her to have a going-away ceremony for it over the garbage bin they'd dragged to the curb for her. I'd bet dollars to donuts she did it for attention and snuck back out to retrieve it before trash collection the next morning.

The facility was adamant about not keeping valuables on the premises. They had enough on their hands without being accused of tossing a two-carat tissue in the trash! I did not blame them one bit. Anything we could do to make it easier on them to care for Mother, Billy Reid and I were all about it! Having been in the restaurant industry, snacks have always been our love language. Right inside the doorway of her room, we kept a huge bowl stocked with candy and other munchies that everyone had access to. Mother would get panicky and a bit claustrophobic, so her door was always left wide open. We purposely chose a room for her right by the nurses' station so she had constant human contact. Plus, she was deaf as a stump, so it's not like the incessant dinging of the call button disturbed her. One day, I popped in to have lunch with her. In the bustling hallway on the way to the dining room, she inquired rather loudly, "Is my butt getting big being here? I swear, everyone who works here has the biggest butt!" *I need to find some healthier snack options for that bowl,* I thought.

She really was living her best life there. I had never seen her more carefree. She spent her days in the community room doing puzzles with the other residents. An amazing recreational therapist named Aubrie did arts and crafts with them weekly. The evening before Prince Harry married Meghan Markle, I found Mother clad in her nightgown and a construction paper headpiece. She said, "Today in arts and crafts, Aubrie helped us all make fascinators. We're going to wear them while we watch the royal wedding tomorrow. If I wake up, that is." I told her if not, I'd be sure to bury her in it so it wouldn't go to waste!

They even had a little cocktail hour once a week. The wine and cheese came out at four o'clock on Fridays so they could clear out in time for dinner at five thirty. Joy, one of the residents, figured out pretty quickly that the best seat in the house was next to Mother. Mother didn't really drink, but she *really* didn't like being left out, so she always had them pour her a glass. Once Joy polished hers off, she always acted surprised when Mother slid her glass over and insisted that she have it. Well played, Joy! Well played!

In the dining room, Mother was assigned to sit with Kippy. Kippy had been widowed for many years and did not have any children. I never once saw her have a visitor. She devoted her life to being an educator at the college level, and sadly, her mind seemed to be unraveling in real time. She and Mother made for ideal supper buddies. Kippy repeated herself nonstop, and Mother couldn't hear a word she said. That was usually a winning combination. Until Mother had had enough. Mother loved the she-crab soup that was served at Nordstrom's cafe on Fridays, so we'd often try to take her some to break up mealtime monotony.

On one of these evenings, Kippy was her usual inquisitive self and kept asking Mother what she was eating. Over and over and over again, she inquired, "Martha, what are you eating? What did they bring you?" Mother replied, "It's soup." Again and again and again. Kippy would ask. Mother would reply. The loop continued for several minutes until Mother couldn't take it any longer. Mother drew the biggest breath I've ever seen her take, and with a beet-red face, bellowed at the top of her lungs, "It's SHHHHHHHHHOOOOUUUUPPPPP!" The entire dining hall turned to see what was going on at our table. I bet it's the first thing some of those people had heard in years! I thought it was hysterical. Kippy was unfazed. She'd clearly forgotten what they were talking about. To this day, we still call it SHHHHHHHHHOOOOUUUUPPPPP in our house!

Each resident had a shadow box on the wall, right outside of their room. Most of the boxes contained a lone photograph of a dashing gent in his military

attire or a blushing bride in her wedding gown.
An image of a lifetime fading around the edges.
It's the original bait-and-switch profile picture. I've
never been on a dating app, as I've been married
since God was a baby, but the stories I've heard are
hilarious. Someone thinks they're meeting Brigitte
Bardot for coffee, and Meth Head Mary awaits with
a caramel macchiato in hand. It's crazy to think
that these wisps of humanity were once-virile hottie
patotties! You cannot moisturize or hydrate enough to
overcompensate for what the future holds.

A few of the shadow boxes remained empty, so I
took it upon myself to decorate them. It truly was an
act of service at the highest level, seeing as I am the
least crafty person on the planet. I think going to a
Michaels Store for craft supplies is akin to entering
the mouth of hell. The rows of mishmash waiting to
be assembled into masterpieces made me feel like I
was breaking out in hives. Maybe there's a reason why
over-the-counter relief from Walgreens can be found
within spitting distance of every location.

I would sneak up on a weekend night after the
residents were tucked in. Armed with plastic you-
name-its for whatever holiday was before us, I'd
entertain myself and transform the entrance to their
rooms to look like Cupid, or a leprechaun, or the
Easter Bunny had paid them a visit. Sometimes it
would look like spring had sprung, or a festive fall,
or a winter wonderland. I always did Joy's, Kippy's,

Dottie's, and Mother's. Mother's, of course, was always a little bit snazzier, a string light thrown in here, a puffier letter there. My greatest delight was watching them try to figure out when, how, and by whom it had happened.

Hospice Schmospice, I'm Outta Here

On Mother's eighty-ninth birthday, we threw her not one, but two, surprise parties. While she was napping after lunch, the multi-purpose room and the wheelchair-bound partygoers were transformed with streamers, banners, potential stroke-inducing—oh lawd, what was I thinking?—flashing necklaces—oh well, what a way to go—hats, noise makers, enough beads to make a Mardi Gras parade proud, and a huge cookie cake with ice cream.

She had two candles to blow out, and it took her eight tries. I think she was out of breath from singing "Happy Birthday" to herself. Yes, I have a video of her singing, "Happy Birthday to Me!" That tracked. It was nice to see that she was still on brand heading into her ninth decade. While the sugar and the attention went to her head, I slipped out of the festivities to go decorate the fancy-schmancy restaurant downstairs where we were expecting a crowd for dinner.

After Mother's party with her mates on the long-term care floor, I wheeled her downstairs under the guise of getting a little fresh air. On our way back up, I told her we should take a peek in the restaurant to see what it was like, as we'd been meaning to make a reservation and just hadn't gotten around to it yet. She was utterly shocked to see a huge table full of family, friends, former employees, and neighbors waiting to celebrate with her.

She said, "Tonya, did you do all of this because you don't think I'm going to be here next year?" And then proceeded to sing Happy Birthday to herself again with the crowd. Then she did something completely out of character. She thanked me and told me she loved me.

I thought, *Oh damn, lady, maybe you're not long for this earth!*

Six weeks later, on Friday, September 27, 2019, Billy Reid came home from his daily visit with her and said that the facility was having palliative care stop by to do an evaluation. She seemed to be withdrawn and no longer trying, often opting for Cheerios in her bed versus dressing and going to breakfast. They thought having one-on-one care for a few hours a day might do her some good. At first, I assumed everyone there was starting to taste like chicken, and she was just ready for some new blood.

I had a meeting across town, and Billy Reid offered to drive me. On our way, he told me to call the nurse's station and ask how the rest of Mother's day was going. Melany, one of our favorites, answered the phone and said the social worker had actually just shown up to see about getting Mother on their schedule starting first thing Monday.

I told Melany we could come by for a minute right then or we would stop by in a couple of hours, as I had somewhere to be. She assured us that Mother seemed fine, to go do our thing, and to come by afterward. We got to the next traffic light and looked at each other. Without saying a word, Billy Reid turned toward Sharon Towers instead of heading to my appointment.

Within minutes, we were in her room. Billy Reid was going over the woman's evaluation of Mother. Mother was lying in bed already, or maybe still, in her nightgown, and it wasn't five o'clock anywhere. She was gazing out the window and had her hands folded on top of her covers. She smiled when she saw me, and I asked her if she'd like me to "do her face."

Doing her face was a little ritual we had where she would squeeze her eyes shut, and I would spray facial toner on her face and goop her all up with moisturizer. She loved it because it felt great, and I loved it because I would always spray her in the face way too many times 'til we both started giggling.

This time was different, though. I still pretended to waterboard her with potion, but while I was massaging her face, I said, "Mother, I want to thank you for how you've always accepted me as a daughter, not just your daughter-in-law. I have thoroughly enjoyed our relationship, and I love you." She opened her eyes and smiled.

At that moment, she looked over my shoulder and noticed Billy Reid talking to the lady. Mother couldn't hear for shit, but she had an eagle eye. She saw the woman's name tag and said, "Am I in hospice?!"

I replied, "No ma'am, not yet. She's a social worker from there, and she's just here to tell us about some options for you to have some new visitors starting next week. There's nothing for you to worry about, though." I told her we had somewhere to be and that we would be back in a couple of hours to stay longer.

As we left, she waved and said, "Bye, Billy."

Sweet Melany texted me two hours later to say that she stayed after her shift because Aubrie, the former arts and crafts director, had stopped by, and they'd ended up visiting with Mother.

She said Mother had been a little anxious since seeing the hospice worker, but was much calmer now. I thanked her and told her we were on our way back. Fifteen minutes later, we stepped off the elevator, and I could see across the way that, for the first time ever, Mother's door was closed. Billy Reid was trailing behind me, as it was his third time there that day.

Out of nowhere, someone on staff I'd never laid eyes on before seemed to take one gliding step from across the room to land in front of me and said, "I'm so sorry. She's gone. I just walked in to check on her, and she's gone."

My brain was not processing what she was saying until I heard Billy Reid yell, "WHAT? ARE YOU FUCKING KIDDING ME? We missed it! Well, gawd damn! The same thing happened with my dad!"

For reference, years earlier, Bill Reid was dying from a glioblastoma brain tumor, and Billy Reid stopped by to see him on his way home from working late at the restaurant one night. He'd told me that he was dog-ass tired sitting at his father's bedside, trying not to doze off. He finally stood up and told his dad he would see him in the morning. Billy Reid then drove exactly seven-tenths of a mile to his house. The phone was ringing as he walked in, family on the other end announcing Bill Reid had passed.

Death can be disarming in the best of circumstances, and Billy Reid and his mother never seemed to reach the best of circumstances. We walked into Mother's room as she lay there in all her disheveled glory. As usual, her nightgown was riding up her backside, one foot was cocked up on the other leg like a supine yogi in tree pose, head back, eyes and mouth open. Her perfect resting position. A position I had warned every caregiver ever, that they would find her in, asleep, looking deader than a doornail every damn time, and it would scare the bejeezus out of them until she popped up, awake.

The CNA was nervously fretting and flitting around the bed, grabbing to straighten up the covers, apologizing for not having had time to make Mother look more presentable for us.

I giggled and said, "No need to put on any airs for us. This is exactly what she looked like. It's oddly comforting. She just looks like she's sleeping."

Billy Reid added, "If she looked any better, she wouldn't look like ours." She probably thought we had lost our minds!

She calmly instructed, "Take your time. Stay with her as long as you like, and when you're done, I'll call for someone from the funeral home to come get her. Have you decided what kind of burial you're going to have so I can let them know for you?"

Billy Reid, still reeling and not ready to take it down a notch, said, "We're gonna burn her!"

I jumped in with, "Alrighty then, it sounds like we're going with cremation!" She knew for certain we'd lost our minds then!

A week later, on October 4, 2019, Martha Jean Robertson Reid was laid to rest. It was as if the doors of hell themselves had opened to welcome her. It was a record-breaking ninety-seven degrees! The heat index registered a whopping one-OH-four degrees under the tent for her graveside service!

Years earlier, Mother had summoned me to her house. She was in a twit and needed my help sorting some things out. Foremost on her anxiety-riddled cortex was getting a tree planted at what would be her final resting place. The tree was only a couple of hundred bucks, but the cemetery required an engraved plaque that cost over a thousand dollars. She wasn't thrilled about the price, and she couldn't decide between the options that were offered.

Forgetting for a moment who I was talking to, I asked, "Well, your parents and your husband are already buried there. What kind of tree did your mother like, or did Bill Reid have a favorite? How would you like to honor them with the engraving?"

She snapped back, "The tree isn't for THEM, it's for ME! It's going to be so hot lying there!"

I laughed and said, "You know you're not going to be there, right? You're not going to feel a thing."

That was also the same day she had me mail a check to the church. I had known her for decades at that point and had never known her to go to church. That didn't stop good ole St. Luke's from sending tithing envelopes to her every month.

Handing the sealed envelope to me, she said, "Here. Mail this for me. Just in case."

I asked, "Just in case, what?"

She answered, "You know," offering nothing else.

"You mean, just in case this is how it works? Like how you get into heaven?" I replied. She nodded her head yes.

At some point during her funeral service, I was kicking myself for not reminding her to plant a frigging orchard for shade, and I was wondering how cheap she'd been with those damn checks!

I found out later that our son Porter was sitting there during her memorial service wondering, *All these people paying their respects, who are they talking about? She sounded great. I sure wish I'd met that lady!*

I guess this tree has her own apple too.

Tissues and Tic Tacs

My good friend, Celia, was lamenting one day about needing to go check on her mother in Florida. It wasn't the checking in part; it wasn't the traveling to Florida part; it was the fact that it was her mother. I could read between the lines and offered to accompany her. "It'll be fun! Come on! I'll be a buffer. How bad could it be?" I said in an attempt to motivate her. She wasn't buying it. The weight on her shoulders was palpable. She proceeded to tell me how I was too busy to go help her and that I had plenty of people and things that I was already responsible for, to which I responded, "Well, you're in luck then, because everyone knows if you need something done, ask a busy person!" Wait, is it a busy person or a busybody? Hmm! Either way, I had her covered!

I happily tagged along with a laptop in hand, looking forward to stealing time to write between chores and errands and conversations and dinners. (I was in the final stages of writing this book.) Plus, what's not to love about a visit to an oceanfront condo complete with a chiweenie mix furbaby named Sassy?! For those unfamiliar with a chiweenie, it's pretty much Mother Nature's greatest example of two wrongs making a right. Two of the most feared, stubborn, and relentless dog breeds on the planet: a chihuahua and a dachshund. It's evolution's way of testing the limits of man versus beast, where humans don't stand a chance!

The trip started off great! In an effort to make it a relaxing experience, I booked us first-class tickets before Celia could protest. The last thing we needed was to be boarding with group number 153 and end up being stored in the cargo hold or the wheel well! I knew my girlfriend needed to show up refreshed and ready for whatever dynamics occurred between her and her mother. She, in turn, had a driving service come pick us up. Being natural caregivers from the "panini" generation, we understood the importance of making the trip as stress-free on ourselves as possible. Plus, there was no way her eighty-eight-year-old mother was going to drive the forty-five minutes to the airport and back to fetch us.

We found her mother, Ann, snug as a bug in the den. She and Sassy were watching TV. Yes, the dog watched TV. I saw it with my own eyes. A dog food commercial came on, and she went bananas! That living, breathing lumbar support popped out from behind Ann's backside, emerging from more pillows and throws than one would think a chair could hold. She was queen of the mountain on the ottoman, barking louder and louder every time a dog appeared on the screen. It had never occurred to me how often dogs are used in marketing campaigns and not just to sell pet supplies. Sassy's interaction was quite enlightening. Apparently, she also enjoyed watching football. As it was February and football season was over, I had to take Ann's word for it.

We went to dinner in the bar area at Ann's country club on Thursday evening. Celia and I enjoyed our meals. Ann, not so much. She ordered the broccoli cheddar soup and a wedge salad. When her bowl was half eaten, I noticed that she was doing a lot of chewing for such a normally smooth concoction. I inquired about her soup, and she responded that it sure had quite a bit of chicken in it. We told her broccoli cheddar shouldn't have *any* chicken in it. Upon further examination, we discovered it was clam chowder. She informed us that she much preferred the red-based Manhattan chowder to whatever she had been served. Her wedge came next, and she was thoroughly unimpressed with the paltry amount of blue cheese dressing and bacon on top of the anemic-looking iceberg. Celia offered to ask the kitchen to correct their culinary mishap, and Ann, in turn, begged her not to say anything. The wine and the key lime pie were all she was really after.

The next morning, I awoke to Ann telling Celia that she had stayed up late when we got home and decided to fire off a scathing email to the club. Ha! So much for not making a big deal about it. They were also talking about finding a ring Ann had lost in her condo some time within the previous year or so. It was a black opal that she and her husband had acquired years earlier on a trip to Australia. I feigned ignorance with Ann so she wouldn't know that Celia and I had already hatched a plan. I knew before we even bought our plane tickets that Celia and her mother were sick over the ring's misplacement. That Celia, Ann, and Ann's friend Sandy had gone through the condo with a fine-tooth comb on several occasions, and that they had turned up empty-handed. Sandy was the sweetest woman I had ever met. A couple of years earlier, Celia had decided to hire her to be her mom's companion. Sandy would walk Sassy, drive Ann to appointments, go to lunch or dinner, run errands, and even accompany Ann and Sassy to Charlotte on occasion to visit Celia.

Our master plan was to rummage through every pocketbook and every jacket in Ann's closet while she was playing bridge. We had approximately four hours to locate the jewel without being caught snooping. We felt so sneaky entering the sanctity of her closet. Celia told me that Sandy, who was there multiple times a week, sometimes multiple times a day, out of respect, never *ever* stepped foot in Ann's room. We were definitely being naughty, but we hoped recovering the treasure would be worth the risk. The only bounty we discovered was tissues and Tic Tacs, maybe an occasional dollar bill. When I say we found tissues and Tic Tacs, I mean that every single solitary purse and pocket yielded at least three Tic Tacs and two tissues. Celia and I were getting giddy. I think all of the dust and deceit were tickling our funny bones. I joked about how someday (a long time from then, of course), Celia would have to pass out tissues and Tic Tacs at her mother's memorial service, as clearly they were two of her favorite things. Celia, thankfully, shares my often inappropriate brand of humor. We oddly had tons of fun, yet also came up empty-handed.

On the way out the door to dinner Friday night, Celia dropped an F bomb, thinking she'd forgotten something, then immediately located it in her bag. Ann exclaimed, "CELIA! Your cursing has gotten so bad!" I let out a guilty giggle and offered, "I think that might be my fault." Ann gave me the side-eye and a tight-lipped, "Mmmmm hmmmm." I promised to behave since we were going to the fancy club dining room that evening.

Once drinks were served, Celia confessed to Ann that we had scoured her closet to no avail. Gratefully, Ann was miffed by the ring's continued absence versus mortified by our intrusion. I told them that I kept feeling like the ring was hiding in plain sight, and Celia kept doubling down on the fact that it was gone forever and that her husband, Bob, could possibly be right about it having been stolen. Not by Sandy, of course! Never Sandy! She didn't have a dishonest bone in her body. *That* was never in question.

We had *the* most delightful evening, and our meals were perfection! Wanting to get to know Ann, I asked her tons of questions about herself. How did she meet her husband? Where did they live after he finished medical school? How did she like it? And so on. I learned that they had been set up by friends. They moved to a small Southern town in Georgia. She made some dear friends there. And it was also the place that reinforced her disdain for anything religious. Settling on the big ole ugly buckle in the Bible Belt will do that to a person. Especially if you imbibe in good company, wine, and speaking your mind.

Celia explained how they didn't have much contact with her father's side of the family since Ann had called one of them a bitch, to her face, at his funeral. Ann, defending herself, said, "She is a bitch!" With mock exasperation I added, "Language, ladies! We're in the nice dining room!" We lost all dignity from there as they delved into family dynamics. I was all ears. It came time for dessert, which Ann and I were all for. With me trying to remain in good grace and her having shared her key lime pie the night before, I wasn't about to suggest I partake in one spoonful of Ann's waffle bowl ice cream sundae, so I ordered the beignets.

As dessert and additional glasses of wine appeared, I said, "Dang it!" because I was trying to be all rated-G, "I forgot to bring Jesus!" Ann looked at me like I had three heads. *So much for me maintaining any ground with her.* Celia jumped in and told her mother that I was working on an idea for another book. I elaborated that as a teenager, I also had moved to the Deep South. I'd been raised Catholic, and when I got to Mississippi, I was immediately met with, "Where do you go to church? Have you been saved? Have you found Jesus?" To which I always thought, *Where did he go? I didn't know he was lost.*

I was also struggling with the current political climate of our country. From what I understood of His teachings, people claiming to follow Jesus seemed to be more aligned with Judas. Pledging piety to Jesus in private and betraying Him in public with a kiss or a vote. Bending the knee to a wannabe earthly king. Guess they can keep wearing their WWJD bracelets. Off my soapbox now.

Needing a creative outlet for my frustration, I decided to order a box of a hundred tiny Jesuses and take Him with me everywhere. I leave Him out in the world, at the post office, in the vast polish holder at the nail salon, in the avocado bins at the grocery store. Because if deportation rates go as promised, I think you'll more likely find Jesus Christ Himself in the produce section than anything that needs picking. I even left Him by a hymnal at a funeral I recently attended to ensure that anyone entering the church would actually find Him there. I take pictures of JC out in the wild in hopes of turning the photos into a coffee-table book at some point. I had intended to bring Him and rehome Him somewhere in the club that evening.

With dessert demolished and decorum deserted, the check came for Ann to sign to her tab. Every check came with chocolates and mini confectioneries for the table. Ann decided she would prefer to take hers home and have them in the morning rather than try to find one more spot in her satisfied belly. When we got home, I placed her treats and one of my Jesus figurines in a small dish covered in plastic wrap. I set them on her table where she would enjoy her coffee the next day and announced, "Here, Ann, you can have breakfast with Jesus." I was met with a good-natured eyeroll and a grin. I had also been teasing Ann that Sassy, who had quite successfully been trying to French kiss me all day, was going to sleep with me. To which her grin faded, and she informed me that Sassy sleeps with her. *Roger that!*

The evening was winding down, and Celia and I were slung up on the sofa, talking about an essay I'd written earlier. She's a voracious reader and is always very supportive of my latest musings. As I was reading aloud, Ann wandered by on her way to get ready for bed. We inquired if we could be of any assistance, and Ann told us that it wouldn't be necessary. We decided we would call it a night as well.

Twice, Sassy burst through the guest room door to get to us, and twice I scooped her up and hurried undetected into Ann's bedroom to toss her onto her rightful resting spot. Both times, I stopped at the edge of the doorway and heard Ann at her bathroom sink getting ready to retire. By the time I got back to our room at the opposite end of these ample accommodations, Celia was already sound asleep. Being a night owl, I grabbed my pillow and computer and made myself comfy on the vast enclosed porch on our side of the condo. I could hear the sounds of my surroundings settling down for the day as my creativity was waking up to write. I heard a door close. I noticed the breeze rhythmically bumping the furniture on the exposed ocean-facing porches that wrapped around the building. I heard nothing that caused me any curiosity or alarm. At some point in the wee hours, I decided to just rest my eyes for a moment, which is code for "I am blissfully cozy and not about to disrupt myself by changing locations."

At eight o'clock the next morning, I awoke to Celia standing over me. In an even tone, she said, "Tonya, wake up. Something bad happened." Without explanation or urgency, she turned around and walked calmly out of the sunroom. I was barely conscious, but I fully understood that I was to follow her. As we weaved our way through the condo, I realized we were headed toward her mother's bedroom. Once there, Celia stopped at the doorway. I was trailing too closely behind her to see anything out of the ordinary. She stepped aside and extended her arm out as naturally and effortlessly as Vanna White revealing a letter on *Wheel of Fortune* and said, "She's dead. I just found her like this." I realized that this time, not making an entrance had little to do with protocol and everything to do with disbelief. There was Ann, lying on the floor. Dead. She had never even made it to bed. We stood at the threshold, stunned, and I whispered, "Something bad *did* happen."

Celia has been a doctor, like her father before her, for nearly thirty years. She is no stranger to death or the dying, but nothing could have prepared her for this. Having been friends for decades, we've had lots of conversations about taking care of aging parents. She was my mother-in-law's physician. She helped us navigate the best care possible for her. She talked me off the ledge more than once when Mother had me at my wits' end. She often supported me best by understanding my irreverent sense of humor, and it was my turn to support her. I covered her mom with a blanket as if she were just taking a little nap, and I fished Sassy out of the bed where she'd had the place to herself for the night. Celia returned from notifying the authorities, and we sat on the floor with Ann and Sassy. It was strangely peaceful. Surreal, yet peaceful.

Celia, processing as a daughter through the lens of a doctor—or maybe as a doctor through the filter of a daughter—poignantly offered, "This is a good death. Right? I mean, my mom wasn't built to suffer. She wouldn't have wanted to be in pain. This is the death we all strive for. We can all only hope to live fully, to a ripe old age, and then just go. Right?"

When you've spent years caring for an elderly parent, wondering what their demise will require of you—buying the trip insurance (just in case) for every vacation, setting up safety nets for them to live at home independently and with dignity for as long as possible, racing to their house if a phone goes unanswered for too long, or sending a neighbor to confirm proof of life, playing through different scenarios of "if this, then that" in your mind, trying to preemptively prepare for their passing—I think it's safe to say that inviting your girlfriend to visit your mom and finding her deceased on her bedroom floor on day three after one helluva last supper doesn't even make it to the top one hundred ways you thought it was going to play out! It felt like participating in one of those Tibetan sand mandala ceremonies, where monks painstakingly focus on creating this intricate work of art with millions of grains of sand, only to have it swept away the moment it's complete, in order to symbolize the impermanent, transitory nature of being.

You might have thought, *Well, fuck! If we're all going to end up on the proverbial bedroom floor, what the hell! I might as well take another glass of sauvignon blanc and the ice cream sundae! And now I have all of this space between my ears to think about a million other things because this parental unit of a sandcastle is about to be swept away to their columbarium. And why did I worry so much about something I clearly had no control over?*

Sitting on the floor in the fog *and* the clarity of the situation, because, yes, two things can be true at the same time, Celia and I locked eyes, with her mother resting for eternity between us. So much was swirling through my brain, and the only response I could muster was, "Do you think Ann is having breakfast with Jesus?"

She whispered back, "I think you and Jesus did her in." Thank the Lord we get each other!

Once the sheriff's department came and the funeral home removed Ann from the premises, I turned to Celia and asked her what she needed. She responded, "We have to find that opal. And we have to get this place presentable for the community to come pay their respects once we figure out the logistics." Knowing that Ann did not want a religious ceremony and that she would much prefer a cocktail party celebration of life, we got busy getting her home of nearly three decades in order.

Besides using humor as a salve, cleaning and organizing are among my other superpowers. Celia was wielding the vacuum in Ann's bedroom when I returned with a garbage bag to get to work. I said, "Okay, Celia. I have an idea. I know how we're going to locate that ring, but Ann isn't going to like it. Not one bit. We're going to do what my very Catholic grandmother would do. We are going to pray to St. Anthony, the patron saint of lost objects." There are multiple ways to call on his help, but we kept it simple.

Standing not even two feet from where we'd found Ann earlier that day, we started praying out loud, "Dear St. Anthony, please come around. Something is lost and cannot be found!"

We chanted it three times, louder and louder each time, adding a dosey doe dance at the end for equal parts good measure and absurdity for the events that were taking place. I always say, "At any given moment, you can laugh or cry, and I am always going to laugh." I find laughter to be as great a release of emotion as crying, maybe even more so. Your face certainly looks better afterwards, and the phrase *is* "the more the merrier," not "the more the cryier"! Then I walked into Ann's bathroom, snapping the trash bag open.

From the bedroom, Celia called out over the roar of the vacuum, "I don't know, Tonya. I think it's gone forever. Bob's right: It's been stolen."

I yelled back in response, "Respectfully, Celia, shut the fuck up! You can't invoke St. Anthony and thirty seconds later negate it. You have to give him a minute, at least." I went straight to a mirrored tray on the vanity. It was cluttered with perfume bottles and ornamentation. My hand landed on a bejeweled dragonfly ring holder. It was dusty, so I was going to rinse it off. That was when I noticed what looked like a pair of thick gold cuff earrings. I slid them off the jewelry holder and onto my pinky. I walked toward Celia and said, "These are cute. What's the story on these?" Everything we had discovered so far had a story or special meaning to it. I quickly transferred them to Celia's extended finger and turned back to my bathroom duty.

She flipped her hand over to see the other side and yelled, "Oh my God! This is the black opal! You found it! I can't believe it! This is what we've been looking for!" It had been hiding in plain sight all along! Right next to the sink, where Ann stood at least twice a day for nearly a year. It wasn't a pair of earrings after all. It was two rings. Both with wide gold bands, almost the same size. One had a huge black opal, and the other had rows of diamonds. Once placed on the tail of the dragonfly holder, gravity did its thing, and the weight of the stones flipped them face down, resting against the mirror, so much so that their reflection remained undetected. That is, until St. Anthony got called into action.

The remainder of our weekend went pretty much like that. Bob, on his end, went into lawyer mode (which he is) and texted us a list of things we needed to be on the lookout for. I had never stepped foot in this woman's home, yet I found myself retrieving important documents with ease. I was "locked in," as they say. I went through every document in her office like a human scanner. I couldn't tell you if she was worth ten dollars or ten million, because I wasn't looking for that. As respectfully as one could possibly rifle through someone else's personal effects, my eyes darted across the top of each paper, only retaining what was necessary, and I mentally said, *Okay, this is an investment account. This is a Medicare statement. This is a tax return. Wait! This looks different. Let me examine further. Oh, it's her last will and testament! That goes in the important pile for Bob. Here's another tax return. Oh, here's her car title. This goes in the important pile.*

Bob remembered that Ann had a safe in her closet and told us we needed to find the combination. He said he thought it was on a sticky note in her bedroom. The day was becoming a life-sized version of that game Concentration, where you flip cards over to make a match, and you try to recall where you saw the mate. I knew I'd seen a yellow slip of paper on her dresser. I found it, but it had something else scribbled on it.

I stood with hands on hips, taking in twenty-seven years of acquisitions. As if guided by Ann herself, I went straight to one of her bedside tables. Behind the sleep apnea machine, a lamp, two flashlights, an alarm clock, and a vase of dusty fake tulips, I discovered an ornate box. I removed the lid and peered inside. I spied a tiny manila envelope, the kind you get at the local hardware store when you buy loose screws. (Yes, I'm fully aware of my word choice here!) I pulled the envelope out, and in it was the combination to the safe.

Moments later, I called for Celia. She found me on the floor of the closet with the contents of the safe in front of me. She exclaimed, "Where did you find *that?*"

I answered, "In the safe."

I could hear Bob laughing on the phone when Celia said, "Bob, Tonya is either an FBI covert operative or a witch!"

I told them, "Just be glad I use my powers for good, not evil."

We left on Monday as scheduled, and it was mind-boggling how much we'd accomplished. Still in a daze at the airport, Celia said, "I have no idea what day or time it is. No clue what the date is."

I pretended to consult my watch and teased, "It's September 532nd. We've been here for almost two years. Our visas to the country of Florida have expired, and it's time to go home!"

The Gift That Keeps On Giving

I can see clearly now that learning to take Mother in stride is the gift that continues to have a ripple effect. It has come in handy over the years when friends and clients have come to me for support in navigating their own snarky relationships. It's amazing the little things I've learned. For instance, when someone croaks, get two dozen death certificates instead of the five they tell you to get, because everyone and their brother wants you to send them one for anything and everything you have to do for the deceased's estate. And they have to be originals! No photocopies.

No matter how desperately someone holds on to their belongings, even if they value their stuff above all else, they most definitely leave that shit behind when they peace out. And nobody wants it! Nope! Madame Alexander dolls aren't worth pennies on the dollar, if you can even find someone who knows what they are. You cannot give a piano away. I know because I made half a dozen calls to schools, churches, community centers, and anywhere else I could think of. But a junk man will pile it on the back of his truck if you drag it to the curb. I mean, or so I've heard! Fine china, antiques, Hummels, tiny spoons from every state, and clocks out the ass! If you want motivation to get a grip on your own acquisitions, go help someone deal with what's left of someone else's lifetime. Or better yet, don't buy it in the first place! The estate sale we had for Mother barely covered the cost of six weeks at a care facility. You'd better believe I'm constantly cleaning out closets around here so my kids won't have to deal with a mess!

It's nice to hear "please" and "thank you." The other day, I overheard our granddaughter Lucy say, "Please," to Billy Reid. To which he replied, "You're very welcome." She said, "You know, Pops. I really like it when people say 'you're welcome.' I don't like it when they don't." Amen, sister. Amen. Try having them "let" you and see how much that gets to you. I'm glad our grandkids didn't inherit that from their great-grandmother. I have always been a stickler for gratitude, and I have a deeper appreciation for expressions of it now.

It's okay to feel how you feel. Billy Reid was really conflicted when his mother died. He didn't shed a tear. Still hasn't, at least not over her. She wanted us to live in her house, which we bought from her estate. At first, Billy Reid was dead set against it. It was where his family had moved when he was in the third grade. He said that he could point out every spot he'd ever had an ass chewing from his parents. Even though it was the right size, a three-bed, two-bath ranch in an ideal location, he wasn't sure he could do it.

It's okay to change your mind. One day, Billy Reid announced that we were, in fact, going to buy and live in his childhood home. His reason being, "We're looking to buy some old bitch's house. We might as well buy our old bitch's house." It made sense to me. Plus, I promised we'd make new, better memories there. It's cathartic to transform a once-unsavory environment or situation into an empowering one. To take ownership, to take your power back, not to rewrite history, but to learn from it and give your story a happier ending. You can love someone, having been thoroughly grateful that you met them on your journey, and it can thrill your soul that you don't have to mess with them anymore.

Two things really can be true at the same time.

Acknowledgments

I want to pile heaps of gratitude on every woman who has helped form who I am today. Even if, at the time, it didn't seem like something beneficial or something to be thankful for. It all sure has come in handy.

Mom, thanks for giving me the space to express myself. That couldn't have been the easiest parenting route to take. My countless aunts—what the heck, let's count them anyway! Terri, Susan, Carmen, Jenny, Barbara, Kathy, Lenora, Mary, Tanya, Michele, Denise, Patti, Sylvia, Becky, and Alice, I have incredible takeaways from each and every one of you. My grandmothers, Gloria and Porter, I thank you for your impact too. Jenn, Tiffany, Loo, and Rachel, thank you for loving our sons. My granddaughters, Lucy and Ruby, you are already solidly certain of who you are, and the future's so bright because of you.

The wise women who were there when I needed you, you are angels sent from above. RIP, Mrs. D and Mary Helen. Mrs. Kerry, thank you for taking me in as one of your own. While I'm at it, I'll even give praise to the nuns at St. Pat's! Mrs. McLaughlin, thank you for your encouragement and the delight you express about my writing.

Anne Henderson, Felicia Kendrick, and Becky Mitchell, thank you for being Mother's dear friends.

My bestie, Shelly, I think we need to record an album together, or at the very least, enter a lip-sync competition. If nothing else, we'd laugh our asses off!

My team and clients at the salon, thank you for the way you took Mother with a grain of salt, welcoming her with open arms. Oftentimes not by choice. But you always rose to the occasion.

Celia, thank you for letting me share your story. I know it's still raw. When the fog clears, you'll see how relatable it is, and that it is exactly what someone out there needs to hear.

Melany Mendoza and Aubrie Re, you were always so kind and patient with Mother. Alyson McGill, you were always such a breath of fresh air, calling Mother's big ass headphones "Granny Beats"!

Everyone at Synergy Publishing Group, eternal gratitude for staying on me to bring this story to fruition, after excavating a completely different book out of my soul to make way for this one. Shana, Cindy, Melisa, Taylor, Lydia, and Mallory, I appreciate you beyond what I'm capable of expressing.

Mother, may you rest in peace. All of your shit is gone, but the best part about you lives on: all of the crazy stories of our adventures together. I wouldn't trade them for anything!

About the Author

Tonya Reid is a hairdresser by trade and a storyteller by nature. As the author of *US Hairways: Snippets from a Hairdresser's Journey* and *You Can't Shoot Your Mother-in-Law: The Entirely True Tales of a Daughter-in-Law,* she showcases her knack for capturing the moments of humor and heart in any situation. She believes that laughter makes the tough times easier and the fun stuff even better.

Tonya lives in Charlotte, North Carolina, with her husband, Billy Reid, and a wiener dog named Dolly, her grand-dachshund she stole from her son. She is grateful for the funny (and not-so-funny) stories of her life that inspire her work. She is even more grateful that her daughters-in-law have never expressed an interest in writing.

Invite Tonya to your book club—she'll likely show up bearing snacks and plenty more stories to tell.

Connect with Tonya for book readings, events, and speaking engagements:

thetonyareid

synergypublishinggroup.com/tonyareid